Barriers to a Better Environment

Barriers to a Better Environment

What stops us solving environmental problems?

Stephen Trudgill

Belhaven Press,
a division of Pinter Publishers
London

First published in Great Britain in 1990 by
Belhaven Press (a division of Pinter Publishers),
25 Floral Street, London WC2E 9DS

British Library Cataloguing in Publication Data
A CIP catalogue record for this book is available from the British Library

ISBN 1 85293 126 4

Library of Congress Cataloging in Publication Data
A CIP catalogue record is available from the Library of Congress

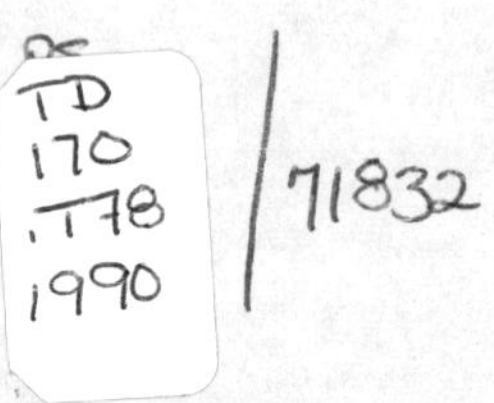

Typeset by Selectmove Ltd, London
Printed and bound in Great Britain by
Biddles Ltd, Guildford and King's Lynn

Contents

For Nige and Lynne

List of Figures

List of Tables

Preface

How can we tackle environmental problems? Can we tackle them better in the future? Can we solve more of them? Why should we bother? These are some of the questions which people often ask when talking about environmental problems, whether it be the destruction of the tropical rainforest, global warming, soil erosion in Africa or pollution of the seas. They want to know why these things are important. If they see something as a significant problem, they want to know what can be done about it. If nothing is being done, they want to know why not.

One difficulty often lies in tracing the origins of a problem. Is there an immediate problem with the actions of an individual, such as a farmer or an industrialist, does it go back to government policies, or do you rapidly get into a discussion about the world economic order? Problems may not be tackled because of local factors or because of much wider policies and attitudes.

This book aims to see if it is possible to make the reasons for not solving problems easier to identify, and therefore to tackle. It is thus a way of looking at environmental problems and how we might tackle them, and it simply asks, *If we think there are things wrong with the environment, what barriers are there which stop us from making environmental improvements, and how can we overcome such barriers?* The book is aimed at people interested in tackling environmental problems; it is not a comprehensive textbook, but a discussion of ideas and conceptual structures for those who are involved in environmental studies, management, policy-making, campaigning and education.

Acknowledgements

I am grateful to many people: Ron Johnston for critical discussion of ideas at an early stage of this book; Tim Burt for asking me to be the environmental columnist for *Geography Review*, from which sprang interviews with Jonathan Porritt and Nicholas Ridley, full of useful insight on the environment; Andrew Lees, of Friends of the Earth (FOE), for insight into FOE campaigns and thoughts on confrontation versus education; Richard Sandbrook, of the International Institute of Environment and Development (IIED), for encouraging discussion at an embryo stage of the book; Anil Agarwal and Sunita Narain, of the Centre for Science and Environment, Delhi, for impassioned critical discussion and insights into Indian environmental issues; Brian Walker for his insights and experience from Oxfam and IIED and for involving me in Earthwatch UK; Peter Walker, Director of Action Aid Ethiopia, who, with Amesias Abraham, showed me something of the reality behind the television images in Ethiopia; Helena Norberg-Hodge for inspiring in me an interest in ecological development in Ladakh; Dingle Smith for early encouragement; and other staff at the Centre for Resources and Environmental Studies at the Australian National University for support and insights during my visiting fellowship there – and especially the late Joe Jennings for the memorable camping trips in the bush; many Field Studies Council staff, especially Nigel Coles, Tony Thomas, David Job, Orlando Rutter, Keith Chell, Sue Townsend, Rob Lucas and Helen Springall, whose friendship and dedication to effective environmental education have both sustained me enormously; my university colleagues for continued support, especially Paul White for answering the phone, Alan Hay for his help and encouragement and for tolerating my writing this book when, as Chairman of the Department, he really needed me to get more research grants and write research papers, and the UGC/UFC for not asking for too many reports on and plans for the research I would have been doing if I hadn't been writing the reports and plans; Graham Allsopp and Paul Coles for doing the diagrams more or less on time; Steve Maddock, Steve Plummer, Deborah Sporton, Louise Heathwaite, Dave Thomas, Liz Thomas, Rob Ferguson, Alistair Kirkbride, Jill Ulmanis, Liz Cole and mum for friendship and support; my late father for his early encouragement to write; Iain Stevenson, a hard-headed publisher, informed critic and supportive friend.

I am especially grateful to Nigel Coles and Lynne White for letters and reports written while cycling through India, Pakistan and China for charity and keeping me mindful of the importance of first-hand experience, local people's viewpoints and environmental education when I felt too beleaguered by administration to find the energy to complete the book – the fact that I have finished it owes much to their infectious dedication and enthusiasm, and therefore this book is dedicated to them for the way their writings landed on my desk, full of astute observations, colourful descriptions, sensitive awareness, thought, reflection, fresh insights and positive attitudes to people and environment, reminding me of shared philosophies and realistic idealism in an otherwise cynical world of increasing academic prostitution, and thus spurring me to carry on.

Finally I should not forget Les Dawson, Tom and Jerry, Blackadder, Barry Norman, Simply Red, Diana Ross, Elton John, The Clash, The Cure, New Order and the Valleyside Garden Centre for welcome diversions from work; and Holly the cat for not attacking the word-processor too much.

Chapter 1
Introduction

Acid rain, the hole in the ozone layer, the greenhouse effect, car exhausts, nuclear waste, water pollution, the destruction of the tropical rainforest, pesticides, whaling, famine . . . Environmental problems are now discussed in the media every day, heightening our awareness of the issues involved. But beyond the awareness and concern which many people increasingly feel, how do we now see our future environment? Is everything being tackled and solved, as some politicians would have us believe, or is everything getting worse? Are we hopeful of achieving some utopian state or are we pessimistic? Will we have pure rain, no pollution, lush forests, abundant wildlife and a comfortable quality of life with pleasant homes, security and the sustainable use of the available resources of the earth? Or will we disappear in a welter of environmental disasters and wars over territory, resources and living space?

We cannot accurately predict the future, but with the diversity of human capacities for exploitation, self-interest and idealism, it is probable that neither extreme will unfold: we are sure to have enough idealism and self-interest to take some more steps towards a better environment, but it is equally arguable that human nature is such that environmental degradation and human strife are also likely to continue. In other words, there are some limitations to what we can realistically achieve in improving the environment. It is difficult to conceive that we will ever give up the struggle for a better environment in a climate of pessimism, but it is equally difficult to conceive that everything will ever be paradise on earth. What we can conceive is that it is possible to improve our environment more and that this will involve not losing sight of environmental ideals while tempering them with realism.

If we accept that there will be not only continued efforts to improve the environment but also limitations on that improvement, we can argue that there is a purpose in highlighting what these limitations actually are. The purpose of this is that it may assist in the process of improvement by making the barriers which impede progress into clearer targets for action.

In this book, therefore, we discuss the possible ways of actually achieving a better environment. This involves tackling a series of questions. Can we agree on what we mean by a better environment? If so, how do we get there? What is stopping us? And how can we overcome the barriers more readily? These are timely considerations because there is now an increasing awareness of the desirability of improvements. A view of a better environmental future is often high on the agendas of political and personal actions. This, it can be argued, is related to an increasing democratisation of information about the possible consequences of various actions or inactions. This, in turn, means that more people, whether teachers, parents, students, politicians, scientists or consumers, now seek to influence the future through education, individual actions, marketing strategies, intervention, legislation and by pressure on those who have influence and power.

These trends mean that societies, and individuals in society, are now facing up to and debating fundamental questions of environmental goals, of the means of achieving them and, most importantly, of how far we can realistically expect to go with changes and reform. A particular focus of discussion is the balancing of green ideals about the environment, and their possible implications for radical changes in society, against pragmatism with regard to human nature, commerce, territoriality, the limitations of knowledge, available technology and the economic organisation of society.

From these discussions, it is possible to identify a great diversity of specific barriers to a better environment. These can obviously involve disagreements over the the ultimate environmental aims and goals of society. There are diversities of opinion as to the scope of environmental problems and solutions – especially as to how far solutions should be radically reforming or adapted to current circumstances. There may be disagreements over what, in fact, constitutes a problem. There can also be limitations on the scientific evidence available for identifying the causes of perceived problems. Then, even if people agree on goals, problems and solutions, the implementation of solutions may meet technological, economic, social and political obstacles. This diversity of obstacles, indeed, in itself forms a barrier because it suggests that we have to be able to address many issues of a diverse nature in a coherent fashion before more progress can be made.

Initially, the book attempts to identify the main groups of barriers in order to provide a framework for discussion (Chapter 2). Then, it attempts to specify and exemplify the diversity of barriers in more detail and to analyse and clarify each group of barriers. Within the confines of a book, one cannot hope to explore every topic in depth as each topic will raise substantial questions which themselves could merit extensive discussion and the input of a wide range of specialist knowledge. Thus, the aim is not one of exhaustive treatment of barriers but one of *identification*. Nor is the intention to provide a rigid framework for action, because many of the barriers can be seen to interact with each other in a rather fluid manner. The aim is to provide a basis for a realistic agenda for action by highlighting the range of possible barriers to a better environment.

Chapter 2
Barrier Identification

In Chapter 1, we indicated that there could be a great diversity of barriers to finding and implementing solutions to environmental problems. We realised that the barriers can interact with each other. In addition, it is likely that they will change with each problem. If we are going to be able to discuss this complexity in any logical fashion, it will be useful to group the barriers in some way. Such a grouping should not be seen as rigid, but merely as a framework for discussion.

We have already suggested that there can be disagreements about goals, aims, means, the scope of solutions and about what is a problem. We also indicated that there can be obstacles concerned with scientific evidence and with technological, economic, social and political factors. This suggests an initial classification consisting of six major groups of barriers – agreement, knowledge, technological, economic, social and political – which we will refer to collectively as the AKTESP barriers (Figure 2.1). A detailed discussion of the AKTESP barriers forms the basis of the rest of this book. Here, it will be useful to outline what barrier identification might involve and also what might be involved in each category of barrier.

In barrier identification, we can ask if each stage in Figure 2.1 impedes progress towards a solution. Difficulties over agreement may be a major impediment. But if the first hurdle of agreement is crossed, we then ask whether or not the next barrier forms an impediment – is there adequate evidence or knowledge? (We may agree that something should be done about a problem, but we may not know what the cause of it is.) But if we do know what the cause is, we then ask whether we have an appropriate technology to tackle it. (We may agree on the problem, know what its cause is, but not have the means to tackle it.) If we do have an appropriate technology, do economic, social and political factors then form the crucial barriers? (We may know what to do, but fail to do it for some reason, perhaps limited money, social constraint or political will.) So, at each stage, we are either pinpointing an impediment or moving on to ask whether or not the next stage forms a barrier.

The barriers will often, but not necessarily, operate in this sequence. Thus, for example, economic, social and political constraints might not

Figure 2.1 The AKTESP barriers which hinder the resolution of environmental problems

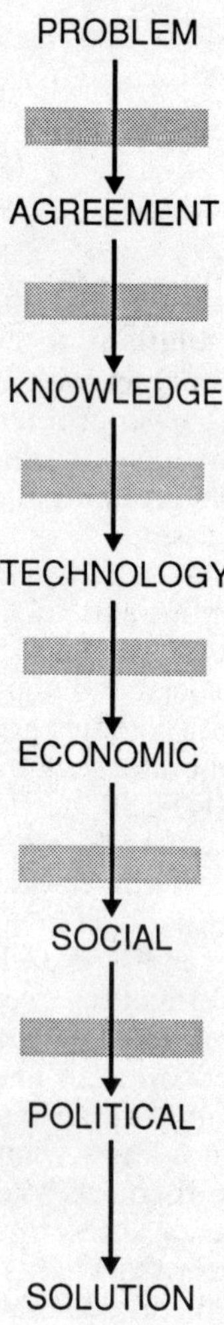

exist but knowledge might be inadequate, that is to say, we may be willing and able to do something but we might not know clearly what to do. The important thing is therefore not to cling to the sequence rigidly, but to use it as a basis for identifying the barriers so that we can ask what exactly it is that is stopping us finding and implementing a solution to an environmental problem, and what are the barriers to a better environment.

Let us now look at the barriers a little more closely. Among agreement barriers we can include the difficulty of achieving consensus about the scope of solutions and the means of achieving them and about ultimate goals. There are also arguments over whether a given problem actually exists at all, what its significance is, what the nature of the problem actually is and whether it matters or not. What one person sees as a problem, another may not; what is seen as reasonable and as an acceptable practice to one group can be unacceptable to another.

Knowledge may be limited about the processes and evidence concerning causes, effects and possible solutions. While we often have some knowledge of basic processes, knowledge has to be reviewed in terms of the ways in which it is gained and used. Inappropriate or insufficient knowledge may mean that we have difficulty in producing effective management plans. It may not be clear how to tackle a problem because we do not have enough knowledge to identify its causes.

Evidence for the existence of a particular effect may not be clear-cut and people may argue over the evidence, possibly according to their prejudices. If the causes and their effects are not clear, it will be difficult to find the appropriate target for the implementation of a solution.

We may also need research at a particular site in order to specify the chain of causes and effects operating at that site. While there might be adequate knowledge about cause and effect processes in general, it may prove difficult to show that these actually operate in particular instances.

Alternatively, the knowledge may be adequate but simply not communicated to those who need it.

But even if knowledge is appropriate and widespread, a lack of technology may then prove to be a major barrier to problem solution. And even if we have a means to solve a problem, the technology might not be appropriate for the social structure or economy of the people involved.

Finally, even if the causes and effects are clear and we also know how to tackle the causes, it may cost too much to do so or it may be socially or politically unacceptable.

These economic, social and political barriers may be the determining factors in tackling environmental problems. But, in stressing the importance of social factors, we must not play down the role of scientific knowledge. Such understanding is a basic requirement of environmental management.

Science is, however, only half the story and must be considered within the social constraints which limit its nature and usefulness.

In the rest of this book we shall discuss each of the AKTESP barriers in turn. If we can identify how they act as constraints to finding and implementing solutions to environmental problems, then we should be able to specify clearer targets for action.

Chapter 3
Agreement Barriers

Insight from India

In the summer of 1988 I went to Delhi to ask Anil Agarwal, Director of the Centre for Science and Environment, what he thought the barriers were to finding solutions to Indian environmental problems. The Centre collates information on the Indian environment and is involved in the formulation and implementation of environmental policy in India. Anil felt that the barriers to a better environment changed according to how you saw the scope of the solutions to environmental problems:

Stephen Trudgill: '*What do you think are the barriers to solving environmental problems in India? What is stopping you solving them? Can you identify the barriers so that you can deal with them? Is it lack of scientific research? Politics? Bureaucracy? Administration? Or what?*'

Anil Agarwal: 'We know what the environmental problems are but I'm not sure that we know what the solutions are. If we knew very clearly what the solutions were, we could identify the barriers to obtaining them. This is because the problems are complex and the solutions relate to a situation where we have to use the same resource base as we already have – and which is going to be under increasing pressure of growing population and growing needs of people – and we have to work out how to use it in a way that will lead not only to greater sustainability but also to higher productivity.'

'*So it's not so much a factor of the biological and physical scientists not coming up with the causes of problems, it's the fact that everything is intermeshed with social problems and social structure?*'

'I think both, because I don't think that the biologists and engineers are really coming up with the answers that are needed to increase productivity on a sustainable basis. Once they do, we will be clearer about what the technical answers are, and then, also, about the social framework that would be needed to make these technical solutions work within a more equitable framework – then we would be able to define what are the social and political obstacles to making them work.'

'*But don't we actually know what a lot of the solutions are? For example, with agriculture, isn't a lot of the answer to finding sustainable resource use one of using more organic matter? Or have you got to have artificial fertiliser to be able to feed the people?'*

'Where is the organic matter?'

'*So is organic matter an answer and the problem becomes getting it? There is an answer but no solution?*'

'Everyone is talking about organic farming and I'm not against it but the point is that nobody has actually sat down and done any exercises to say, yes, organic farming can feed a billion people. When I pose this kind of question to organic farmers they can never give me many sums and say that this will be able to feed a billion people. We need sustainable systems for increased but sustainable productivity. Now it's quite possible that we can do it – having increased and sustainable productivity at the same time. Whether it is from the green revolution side (new high-productivity crop strains, for example), or from the organic farming side, I don't know. The point is that when it comes to these hard issues, if you have to feed in the next five years so many more millions of people, can you get the necessary productivity? Increases will be required. Once I know the technology, then I will be able to say – then there will be answers. Then we can say that this technology demands a certain formal social framework, a certain social discipline to make it work – then I will be able to give you some answers about it, but I can't at this stage.'

'*Going back to the question whether one knows the answer, surely with water pollution, we know that there are technical solutions which exist, although it may be difficult or impossible to implement them, within the social context.*'

'Considering the limited issue – that I have a lot of polluted water coming out at the end of an urban industrial system and I want to clean it up – then, of course, there are lots of available technologies within the Western world and we could easily import them and develop them in an action programme and push our industries to set up these kinds of systems. We can think of subsidies and incentives for industry, on the one hand, and use environmental pollution control laws, etc., on the other – and jail industrialists if they don't submit themselves to environmental protection laws.

However, the point is that it is not enough just to look at water coming out of the end of the urban industrial system. We have to ask wider questions about the the urban industrial system itself in relation to scarce water resources – then you start looking at altogether different questions. Then you might ask why we should be using a sewerage technology which then creates all this polluted water in the first place. Is this the only way to dispose of water – just because some stupid Britishers thought so 200 years ago – and they had to carry away a little bit of solid matter with so much water. I think it is the most classically nonsensical technology ever invented – I'm sorry to use these phrases, but that's how engineers think. The result is that to provide all that water for toilets in cities, they say that we have to dam up the Himalayas.

What we should be thinking about is what could best be done with the water which is available, and questioning whether its use for sewerage is a good one. If we did not use all this water for sewerage, then the problem of dams would disappear, or at least become moderated to a tremendous extent, and at the same time the need for water disposal and the need for pollution control would disappear. So the whole issue is: what is the question you are asking? If you start asking the more fundamental question about overall water use, rather than the limited question about pollution control, then I think what you probably need is a programme for a composting toilet which uses no water for flushing solid waste away.

In addition, the problem facing the municipality is one of low municipal incomes. One of the problems with pollution-control technology is that the municipal corporations here are not able to make the kind of investment necessary because the bulk of the people they are dealing with are very poor and thus municipal taxes are very low. So pollution control itself raises the problem of the need for subsidies for it. If you had a simple composting toilet, every household could build one and afford one and the problem would then be the dissemination of the technology and of the available land – so you would have a rather different set of solutions and problems in achieving them.'

'*So instead of looking at water pollution as a part of sewage treatment – which is treating an effect rather than a cause – you should go back and look at the fundamental causes of pollution in the overall system*?'

'Yes, and that's just one example. You can look at any question that you ask in the environmental field and keep stepping backwards and ask whether there is a larger question behind it. Then, if there is, the direction in which you want to move may be totally different and the obstacles would be very different. So you've got to look at how far back you go in the system, I think, before you can specify the solutions and the barriers to implementation.'

Fundamental or limited solutions?

The Scope of Solutions

The discussion of the Indian environment shows that specific barriers to environmental problem-solving can change according to how the scope of the problem and its solution are viewed. Also, disagreement on the scope, in itself, forms a significant barrier. Thought has to be given to whether the scope of the problem is a more *fundamental* one of enhancing the sustainability of resources and society in an integrated fashion (for example, addressing the overall use of water resources in India), or whether the problems are seen only in much more *limited* terms (for example, tackling water pollution *per se*) and adapting to wider circumstances which are accepted as unalterable, rather than tackling the circumstances as part of the problem-solving exercise. Are the fundamental causes and sources being controlled or are we merely limiting the effects?

We can think of many examples other than those of sewerage and agriculture which Anil Agarwal talked about. If environmental pollution is being caused by an industrial process, a solution might be to propose that the process is improved. However, a more fundamental solution might be to ask whether the industrial process is needed in the first place. Similarly, there is much discussion over the best way to increase future energy production, be it by solar, nuclear, coal, wind or tidal power; a more fundamental approach is to ask whether there is a need for continued expansion of energy production and whether energy conservation could be improved and thus energy needs reduced. The scope for tackling an acidified lake in Norway might be local, with a target of neutralising the acidity of the lake, or wider, with a target of tackling sulphurous emissions from industry in Europe as a whole or the even more radical one of looking at the need for industry at all.

The resolution of a problem thus rests, to a large extent, upon the important stage of the specification of the problem. Is the problem simply one of pollution by waste or of alternative energy sources, or is it one of the actual need to produce waste or increase energy supplies? Who is a solution for? An immediate sufferer, the nation, or what?

Clearly, as the scale of problem specification varies, so will the scale of target definition and solution implementation. The scale can involve the global context and general ideals, such as sustainability. It can also be one of a national scale, a regional scale or a group or individual scale. In addition, local or parochial solutions may cause, or leave unresolved, problems for other people, and wider, more global, solutions may cause other problems for specific individuals or groups.

Of particular interest in these contexts is the *nimby* syndrome. Here, problems of widespread origin, such as the disposal of national nuclear waste at a particular local site, may meet local responses of 'not in my back yard', which only shovel the problem on to another local site. These problems clearly need not only a national view of the best site, which is also acceptable to local people, but, more fundamentally, the problem needs to be balanced within a holistic approach to the need for the action in the first place, the need for nuclear energy at all in relation to the alternatives and the relative desirability of their respective environmental implications. It is only the overall view of energy needs in society which can provide realistic solutions which also stand a chance of general acceptance – rather than partial and separate views of solutions from respective *nimbys*, coal boards, electricity generating boards and the nuclear power lobbies.

Solutions and Goals

We can now see that a given set of problems might require *control* solutions, relating to more fundamental goals involving causes and sources, or *adaptive* solutions, accepting certain situations, frameworks, infrastructures or problems and then working within them. Such solutions can also be seen as *local*, *partial* or *parochial*, or as *regional*, *national* or *global*. We can also see that we need to consider our discussion of solutions in the context of the relationship between defining goals and the scope of the solution. In short, there can be a hierarchy of goals which influences the solutions. Figure 3.1 shows the relationship between the factors involved. The scope of the solution and the specification of the problem will be closely related to goal definition. In addition, the situation is interactive in that limited goals restrict both the problem specification and the scope of the solution and, also, the limited scope of a solution can result in the perception of further problems and a restating of goals.

A look at current and past attempts at problem-solving shows up the complexity of the questions as to what a solution is and for whom. Answers to these questions have varied considerably in scope. Also, the solutions themselves have often been limited. It can be argued that effective solutions for the future should bear in mind the following points and ideals:

1. Solutions are related to *goal definition* and thus goals must be carefully evaluated. Here, it is suggested that solutions should be sought in terms of the fundamental goals of enhancing the resource base of the world and the life it supports – both for its intrinsic value and for our own benefit, seeing the latter two as coinciding in the long term.

2. Solutions are related to *problem specification* and thus problems have to be carefully evaluated. Here, it is suggested that solutions should be fundamental by addressing causes and sources (control strategies) rather than merely dealing with effects (adaptive strategies), though the latter are often more feasible in the short term and within existing administrative structures.

3. Solutions are related to *target definition* and thus scientific research should be directed at establishing causes and sources, as well as the evaluation of alternative strategies of solution. This endeavour should take into account not only the physical, chemical and biological processes involved but, equally, the economic, social and political processes involved. Thus the outcome should be to establish not only the actual environmental components to be targetted but also the institutional components.

4. Solutions should embrace the ramifications of their *implementation* in terms of co-ordinating their effects not only between various sectors of the economy, society and politics within nations but also, for many problems, between nations.

5. Solutions should not be partial in their *scope* in the sense of benefiting one group to the detriment of another. They should,

Figure 3.1 The relationships between goals, problems and solutions

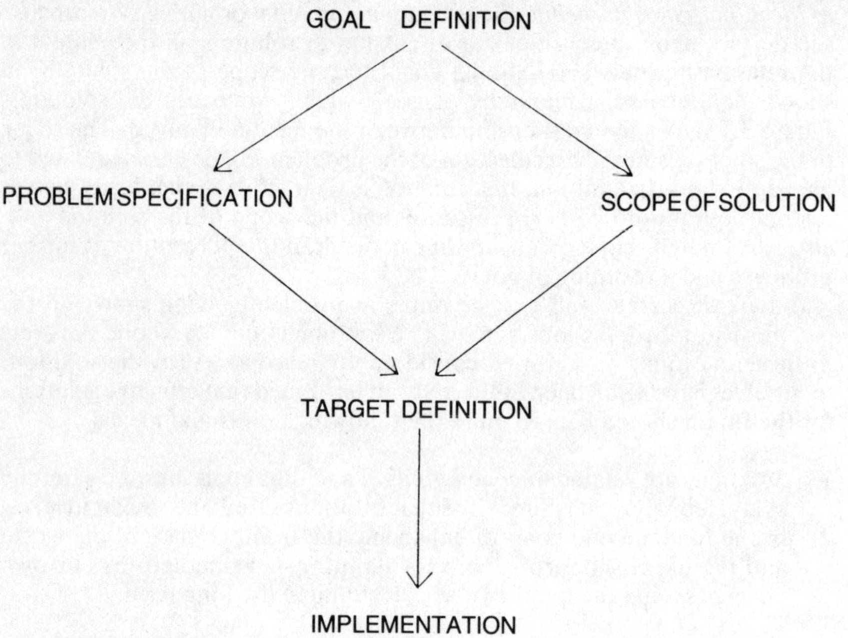

through resource conservation, and at least in the long term, benefit everybody, or the greatest possible number of people, in an equitable fashion.

The interesting questions are how far we go in the hierarchy of goals and solutions and how far we can go within present organisational frameworks. Basically, the question is whether one can accept existing economic, social and political orders and work on adaptive solutions or how far more fundamental control solutions involve changes in such orders. Both these extremes have their detractions. Adaptive solutions may merely displace the problem elsewhere and fundamental solutions may lead to unacceptable social, economic and political upheaval if they are rapidly implemented.

It can be argued that a move from adaptive to fundamental solutions is desirable. However, being realistic, it is evident that making this move socially acceptable will take time and involve an evolution of awareness, gradual institutional reorganisation and progressive goal reorientation through education and the provision of information. The first step in this process is to try to overcome the barrier of disagreement about environmental goals.

Agreeing on Environmental Goals

A Diversity of Goals

Goals may be exploitative and not include environmental objectives and ethics, or they may involve environmental improvement. A lack of agreement on goals can be simultaneously a cause of problems and a barrier to solving them. Furthermore, even if environmental goals are evident, a difficulty can arise in agreeing how to translate agreement on general goals into actions in specific instances and contexts. We can therefore begin our discussion of goals by considering the existence of a range of goals, and the reasons for this range, and then consider how we might agree more on our environmental goals and apply them in real-world situations.

A general environmental goal which is often agreed on is that if the resource base of the planet, and the life it supports, are being damaged, then surely we must try to minimise the damage. This must be in our own interest, not only because we are part of the life which depends on that resource base but also because of our responsibility to other life forms and the ecosystems that support them.

This responsibility should not be borne lightly because we, the most powerful species on earth, have the capability to destroy, create, modify and otherwise affect the ecosystems of the planet, their life forms and our own future. Concern for the environment must, then, surely follow if we agree on general ideals, in terms both of self-interest and of our stewardship for life on earth.

It is, of course, unlikely that the human race can share one common point of view and so such agreement will never be complete. For example, there can be a feeling that environmental matters are a luxury, to be 'fitted in' after we have sorted out other human problems like poverty, health and famine; somehow environmental matters such as conservation can be seen as conflicting with development, so that it is a question of environmental matters *versus* people.

While this feeling may have dominated in the past, a feeling has grown since the 1970s that this is very far from the case and, indeed, that the opposite is in fact true – that our well-being is inextricably linked with the quality of the environment. Not only can human problems, like overpopulation, be a cause of environmental degradation, such degradation can be a cause of human problems, such as famine and poverty. There is thus now a greater measure of agreement that there is a common interest between looking after the environment and looking after people. Indeed, they are now frequently seen as one and the same thing since it is more widely realised that we depend on the environment for our well-being. It is also more agreed that the environment also depends on how we treat it and so we are in an intimate cycle of environmental and human relationships, with a mutual dependency between environment and people (as, for example, described by Harrison, 1987, for Africa).

If we now agree more that tackling environmental problems is important because they involve both our livelihoods and our responsibilities, we then have to ask why we continue to have environmental problems. Do we not agree enough that we are damaging ourselves and life on earth? We often do, but one reason for continued environmental problems is the residual effects of past attitudes. Concerns such as economic growth, human wealth and territory which dominated over environmental concerns, have often left a legacy of environmental degradation. There are two aspects of this legacy – the actual detrimental effects on the environment, and the persistence of entrenched non-environmental, exploitative attitudes – and both of these have to be tackled.

In addition, we have to ask whether newer environmental attitudes are only lightly laid over older ones, and whether they can be brushed aside easily. Current attitudes which stress environmental concerns may be only paying lip-service to them and, while more people now appear to agree on environmental goals, these goals may be subsumed by more immediate interests when it comes to specific actions which challenge older entrenched attitudes and interests.

Another reason is the hierarchy of goals – personal, corporate, national and global. Disagreements over goals can be seen to stem from the potential conflict between limited personal goals and wider global goals. There may be agreement on the wider ideals for global goals – self-sufficiency, resource conservation, wildlife protection – but when these conflict with personal goals such as survival, wealth and livelihood, this can be a source of environmental degradation if the personal goals are exploitative. This differential of goals can be a major source of environmental problems, so understanding this differential and pointing out how personal goals need not be inimical to wider ideals – and indeed how personal goals can be enhanced by nesting them in wider environmental goals – forms a major target for environmental enhancement.

Goals and Contact with the Environment

If we are to have a better understanding of the nature of personal goals, then it is necessary to explore in greater depth how people relate to the environment. In many ways, this involves the immediacy of the relationship: if the relationship is a detached one, it can be argued that personal goals might not involve environmental ideals; but if the relationship is more immediate, then the dovetailing of personal goals and the quality of the environment is more likely to be achieved. We can argue that entrenched, negative, exploitative attitudes – and the associated limited and non-environmental goals – stem from a lack of sufficient contact with the natural environment. So we can propose a basic argument that, *fundamentally, a reason why there are environmental problems is that people have often lost touch with their natural environment and so do not necessarily see the immediate consequences of their actions. Such a detachment leads to the dominance of non-environmental goals. The existence of non-environmental goals then gives rise to environmental problems. Thus, such goals represents a major barrier to a better environment and need to be reorientated environmentally as a first step in addressing environmental problems.*

Early Man lived in close association with the natural environment and so enjoyed an immediate relationship with it. Throughout history there has been a gradual detachment from this close association, and while many agricultural and peasant societies have remained in close touch with their surroundings, the concentration of people in cities has meant that many now live in artificial environments. They are not immediately conscious of the effects of their material consumption and how waste is disposed of. Food and material goods come from shops and wastes are removed from sight, so that urban-dwellers relate only to a diffuse 'somewhere else'. Buying bread does not make them aware of the production process – they did not sow and gather the grain. People in an urban society do not themselves have to deal with such things as sewage disposal and its possible environmental effects. They rely on organisations over which they have no personal control. They rely on relayed information rather than direct involvement for awareness of the consequences of their actions. There thus can be a perception barrier between people in urbanised societies and the natural environment. We may use an aluminium can but whether we throw it away or send it for recycling depends not only on the provision of recycling opportunities but also on the availability of information which may or may not make us aware that the aluminium could have originated in an area where rainforests have been cleared and destroyed in order to excavate the alumium ore – we did not have to dig it out and make the can for ourselves. Thus, our values relate to the usefulness of the object and not necessarily to its environmental relationships. Here, then, the process of education is vital in making us aware of these relationships because we have no first-hand experience of them. This is a fundamental aspect in the origination, and therefore also in the tackling, of environmental problems.

We, if we are urbanised individuals, relate more to the production system which intervenes between us and the environment than we do to the environment itself. Thus the values inherent in the production system form a crucial factor in the avoidance or origin of environmental problems. A problem may have arisen from an exploitative system which uses environmental resources in a way that the exploiter sees as entirely legitimate: there is a market demand and the developer can make a living from meeting this demand. The consumer may or may not then be aware of the consequences of this exploitation, or may be aware but choose to ignore any consequences because there is no necessary direct involvement in the effects of these consequences.

So a fundamental origin of environmental problems lies in a detachment from the environment and this results from the intervention of the production system between us and the environment. As well as a source of problems in itself, this argument is relevant to our discussion on the lack of agreement on goals because the goals may relate more to our immediate surroundings than to any wider issues. It also means that wider goal orientation becomes heavily reliant on secondary sources of information for our awareness of the effects of our consumption on the environment, of other people's goals and of wider concerns about goals of global sustainability.

In recent years, awareness of the environmental consequences of our actions has been substantially promoted by the media, by environmental pressure groups and through more formal education. However, environmental themes in the media tend to find a self-selective audience; for example, natural history programmes on television are watched by those who already have an interest in wildlife. Thus, the environmental content of more generally viewed news bulletins needs enhancement to raise awareness in the environmentally indifferent.

In formal education in schools, although the importance of environmental issues is beginning to make an impact on education syllabuses, it is still the more immediate demands of production and consumption that tend to dominate what is taught – and hence also tend to perpetuate a non-environmental goal orientation of people. More changes in both formal and continuing education are thus crucial in raising (or indeed creating) environmental awareness in those people who are detached from the environment. H.G. Wells, put it dramatically when he said that 'the continuation of civilisation in an acceptable form is a race between education and catastrophe'.

This argument leaves out the question of those who remain in intimate contact with the environment yet can still be seen to be involved in causing environmental problems. Peasants tilling the soil on a steep slope can easily see the soil erosion on that slope. However, while they are less detached from the environment than urban-dwellers, the same underlying reasoning about goals, and their reorientation through secondary information, is also involved here. In addition, the influence of the detached urban-dweller is an important consideration.

First, in reality, peasants might see very few alternatives to taking such actions. Food scarcity, insecurity of land tenure, the need to look after a growing family and other such factors may render it imperative to take such actions for the sake of simple survival, even if it is realised that the action may be damaging. In this sense, there exist comparable clashes between limited, immediate personal goals and wider environmental goals.

Second, although the peasants are less detached from the environment and the environmental consequences of their actions, they may have a poor understanding of the links between actions and consequences. They may be similarly reliant on secondary information through advisers or the media for awareness and goal reorientation.

But third, and most fundamental, their actions can be seen as no more than consequence of policies (or lack of them) which stem from urbanised centres and which have the same detached insentivity to consequences that we have already discussed. Tackling widespread food insecurity, land reform and birth-control programmes usually requires some centralised effort. It is only when the consequences of not undertaking these actions are brought home to a more detached urban bureaucracy, which is willing to listen and act, that things can be made better. This does not deny the importance of local groups which have sprung up when villagers or farmers have taken action because they are only too well aware of the damage they may be doing, but, in general, they are merely acting out the consequences of policies devised by detached urban-dwellers. These policy-makers should therefore be a target for goal reorientation as much as the people who are more in touch with the environment.

Goal Reorientation

A basic difficulty with any goal reorientation, however, relates to the discussions about the scope of solutions we have already undertaken. One can obviously envisage limited solutions which involve a direct approach to the farmers involved and/or a more fundamental approach addressing the urban bureaucracy and the terms of trade between the urban and rural components of the economy. Again, there is a hierarchy of specific goals and objectives involving the well-being of individual farmers, agricultural production objectives and the national economy.

A further difficulty is that people may not be used to thinking in terms of problems and of cause and effect. For example, soil erosion may just 'happen' and not be seen as a problem. Here, the detachment argument does not apply and it is more a matter of how people interpret their surroundings. If something is seen as 'natural' or just simply as 'always occurring' (as described by Blaut *et al.*, 1959), there will be no goal of tackling it and will take an outsider to break the cycle of inevitability. Here, we may be involved in the difficult question of the reorientation of the goals of one culture by another, and the associated importation of views of cause, effect and problems to a culture that does not think in these terms – with all the attendant moral problems of appearing to know best, cultural imposition, denying traditional values and interference with equally valid but different world views. It is difficult for outsiders not to impose preconceived notions about goals and about what constitutes a problem. To attempt to work sensitively alongside people and to see things through their eyes, values and goals, asking them what their priorities are and then helping facilitate them is a skilful art (let alone trying to deal with a personal goal that an aid worker may have in 'feeling useful'!). There is a difference between what could be seen as a posture of knowing best but achieving what you want through the route of discussion and negotiation and a procedure of actually appreciating what the goals of different cultures are and then serving them by the transmission of information to people which they themselves may or may not decide to use in their own way.

Goals and Environmental Problems: Summary

Lack of agreement on goals can represent a substantial barrier to solving environmental problems. There may be agreement on environmental ideals which give us general goals concerned with environmental enhancement and human well-being. However, there are then basic points about hierarchies of goals and about urban-dwellers and decision-makers being seen as detached from the environment and the consequences of actions. Some people are not aware that problems exist, or are not aware that they matter. Others are simply being pragmatic or opportunistic and are concerned with making an immediate living in a difficult and competitive world and see environmental consequences as secondary considerations. These ranges of attitudes and perceptions can be seen as fundamental in causing environmental problems in the first place. If this is so, then they form substantial barriers to tackling environmental problems and they need to be addressed before progress can be made. It becomes clear, then, that goal reorientation is an important process, often relying on secondary information, and involves addressing the difficulties of cultural imposition.

We are aware that tackling problems involves improving the awareness of problems through information and the awareness of consequences of actions in a culturally sensitive fashion. It also involves improving opportunities and security in an otherwise difficult world. But while we need to discuss further how this might be done, we also have to be able to decide what direction we want to go in when we are tackling problems. What do we want to achieve? Given that we have argued that goals are both important and complex, how do we clarify them? Indeed, if we cannot clarify our environmental goals, their diversity and limited scope will remain as substantial barriers to environmental improvement.

Clarifying Our Goals: The Sustainable Use of Resources

We may regret the fact that we have become distanced from our environment by urbanisation and the organisation of the production system, but what can we agree to do about it? Do we wallow in nostalgia about how things once were, or do we try achieve realistic goals? Do we try to realise where we are now and to work from there and then set the goal of returning to a state of greater contact with the environment? Do we try to learn from the study of peoples who are still in close contact with the environment, to see what it is we are missing and then set the goal of trying to build this into our own present situation?

Accounts of people who have close contact with their environment – for example, Laurens van der Post's (1957; 1961; 1976) accounts of the Kalahari Bushmen's spiritual intimacy with all that surrounds them

– shows us that modern man has become spiritually divorced from the environment and impoverished by this process (though this cannot be entirely true, otherwise there would be no environmental movement at all!). But can such accounts help us clarify our goals? The answer is, only if we realise that we have to start from where we are rather than from where we might be.

Some individuals can, of course, aim to escape and find a lifestyle more akin to that of people with a close contact with the environment and of our forebears. But the truth is that society in many parts of the world is organised, industrialised, urbanised and geared to production and consumption; our goals should therefore take the current position of the great mass of people into account if we are to be egalitarian rather than escapist. So while we should try to cherish those societies who are still more in tune with their environment, because they have a moral right to exist in the way they know, we cannot all imitate them, even if we all wanted to – there are too many people.

So we have to start by realising where we are – overpopulated, exploitative and productive – and then clarify our goals by identifying the essence which societies such as the bushmen possess and which we are lacking but which we can realistically adopt. *This essence is that such societies are self-sustaining in relation to their available resources.*

This is the clear message of the writings of Laurens van der Post on the Bushmen. Their lifestyle, consumption of resources, social structure, population levels and culture were all attuned to each other at the time of his writing. We cannot ourselves go back to that precise form of society – and indeed it has been substantially lost itself since van der Post's books appeared. But the message we get, and that from similar writings about Amazonian Indians and other societies which are not detached from their natural environment, is one of adjustment to available resources. This is something which we seem to have lost in our detachment, and, while in no way can we envisage a rapid return to that kind of society, we can at least adopt the principles involved more in an urbanised society, even with its detachment from the environment.

Thus, even given environmental detachment and reliance on secondary sources, our fundamental endeavour in tackling environmental problems is to move to a more self-sustaining system where our consumption is matched by the renewable resources of the earth. This stance gives us a clear agenda of attempting to merge individual goals with overall goals – something which urbanised societies may learn from a study of other cultures. For example, the mass of urban consumers can practice resource husbandry through individual actions, such as recycling and choice of produce, and, given that intermediaries exist between us and the environment, by having the goal of influencing the intermediaries in order to decrease environmental and ecological damage. Conversely, corporate goals can be to enhance the environment and well-being of individuals.

But even if we agree on a general goal of having a self-sustaining society in relation to its available resources, can we agree on how to clarify this goal in specific detail?

Implications for environmental issues

A basic concept of sustainable development is to use resources at a rate at which they can be renewed. The specific details and implications of this concept can be complex and are discussed at length by many authors (most usefully by Redclift, 1984; 1987). In simple terms, however, we often take from, add to, or replace or modify environments in a way that damages the life-supporting resource base of the planet and decreases the self-sustaining quality of that resource base. Table 3.1 categorises some environmental issues under these three headings.

This categorisation is useful since, in the case of taking, extraction or exploitation, it raises the issue of setting goals of either husbanding renewable resources, like fish and forests, to assure a constant supply over time, or, in the case of non-renewable resources like oil and coal, finding alternative sources which are renewable or recycling the non-renewable ones, like aluminium and iron and steel (see Fernie and Pitkethly, 1985).

In adding, we can set the goal of minimising the additions, by control at source and by the redesign of industrial and other processes in the case of pollutants, or by birth control in the case of overpopulation, so that resources are not damaged or used outside their limits.

In the case of replacing, it is more difficult to see how the goal of sustainable resource use translates. While we can try to evaluate environmentally desirable states in terms of self-sustainability, value judgements become involved here about what we may mean by minimising environmental damage and providing pleasant places to live in. Often, however, when habitat change is involved, the criteria of habitat diversity and species richness can be used since it is often argued that diverse areas are more stable and self-sustaining, especially in the face of any change. In diverse areas, the argument is that there is a greater pool of variations which has a greater potential for adaptation to different conditions (see MacArthur, 1955; a counterargument by Hurd *et al.*, 1971; and the review of Pickett and White, 1985).

We can thus set a general goal of a self-sustaining world where the more specific goals are of recycling, husbanding or finding alternatives to non-renewable resources; we can set goals of clean water, air and seas, and we can aim for pleasant, species-rich, self-sustaining productive environments.

Implications for policy: the Brundtland Report

Self-sustainability is the key concept in a significant assessment of the environment written by the World Commission on Environment and Development (1987), chaired by Mrs Gro Harlem Brundtland, Prime

Table 3.1. Categorisation of environmental issues

TAKING	ADDING	REPLACING
ozone hole	acid rain	destruction of the countryside
overfishing	ozone pollution	confier plantation
forest destruction	car exhausts	habitat change
soil erosion	lead pollution	drainage
whaling	heavy metals	urbanisation
mining	radiation	
	greenhouse effect	
	pesticides	
	nitrates	
	water quality	
	eutrophication	
	sewage	
	waste disposal	
	overpopulation	

Minister of Norway, and thus referred to as the Brundtland Report. In trying to find some answers to the question whether we agree where we want to go, we can but be encouraged by this report. The important thing about it is that it is written not by environmentalists but by a group of politicians. The fact that they perceive the problems and the possible solutions is the real milestone in environmental issues. The fact that they can agree on the problems and needs is encouraging. The limitation is that they are not often clear about how their goals can be achieved. However, as we have said, agreement on goals is a necessary but not sufficient first step towards a better environment. The report covers environmental priorities under several separate headings which are summarised (Table 3.2) from digests of the report published by the International Institute for Development and Environment (IIED, 1987) and from *Geography Review* (Trudgill, 1988), beginning with the crucial aspect of sustainable development.

Sustainable development is defined as '*development which meets the needs of the present without compromising the ability of future generations to meet their own needs*'. The report offers seven goals for sustainable development policies:

1. *Reviving growth in areas where it is needed.*
2. *Changing the quality of growth so that growth is more sustainable.*
3. *Meeting essential needs for jobs, food, energy, water and sanitation.*
4. *Ensuring a sustainable level of population.*
5. *Conserving and enhancing the resource base.*
6. *Reorientating technology and managing risks adequately.*
7. *Merging environment and economics in decision making.*

The specific implications of the goal of sustainability come under the headings of population and human resources; achieving food security; the urban challenge; energy; industry; species and ecosystems; managing the oceans, Antarctica and space; and institutional and legal changes. These are detailed in Table 3.2.

We can see from Table 3.2 that the goals are sustainability; the provision of food security; conservation and enhancement of the resource base; and the blending of environmental considerations with economic ones. It is clear that an exploitative economic approach which decreases the self-sustainability of the environment harms itself in the end, and that sensible environmental programmes and a sustainable economy go together.

We have now discussed the barrier of difficulties in agreeing on goals, especially in terms of the differing goals people and groups may have. But we have also seen that it is possible to propose a general goal of the sustainable use of resources and then to look at the implications of this goal for specific environmental issues and policies. If we can overcome the barrier of goal agreement by the development of the points outlined above, we will be nearer to making actual progress towards a better environment. However, further agreement barriers also exist, not only of agreeing on the wide issues of the scope of solutions and on goals, but also in terms of the more detailed issue of defining and specifying individual environmental problems.

Agreeing on Problem Specification

Agreement on problem specification has several dimensions, each of which can act as a barrier to progress. Agreement barriers include agreement on whether a condition, situation or state exists or not; whether a situation represents a problem or not; and whether a problem is significant or not. We can illustrate these dimensions by reference to three environmental issues – ozone depletion, nitrate and lead – as shown in Tables 3.3 – 3.5

What can learn from these examples? In each case, establishing that some pattern, effect or state exists is not especially difficult. What the effects of these conditions are can be debatable. Specifying the exact problem is more complex and involves varying agreement on whether the problem is significant as well as on what the causes of the problems are (which is discussed, together with solutions and other barriers, in later chapters). It can also be suggested that the problem specification involves some perceived harm to people's health and/or to environmental resources. It therefore emerges that concepts of the sustainability of resources, aspects of human self-interest and challenges to value systems are all involved in agreeing on what is a problem. It is also clear that problems can exist because of differing interests – between, say, farmers and the water industry. This means that we have to agree not only that a problem exists and is significant but also that wider health and environmental

Table 3.2 Objectives of the Brundtland Report

Population and Human Resources

* Limit *population growth* by contraception.
* Improve the *survival rates* of children by the provision of medical workers and clinics for both cure and prevention.
* Increase *literacy* to teach the community about the conservation of local soils and water and reversing deforestation.
* *Local communities* must be given a decisive voice in the resource use in their area.

Acheiving Food Security

* Management of the global food system to increase *food production* by 3–4 per cent per year: birth-control measures will take time to be effective.
* Third World governments must turn the *terms of trade* in favour of farmers through pricing policies for food crops, investments in agriculture, support services and marketing.
* Integrated *rural development schemes*, with land reforms and redistribution.
* Governments should *classify land* into three types:

(1)	enhancement areas,	capable of sustaining intensive cropping and high population;
(2)	prevention areas,	fragile areas not to be used for intensive agriculture;
(3)	restoration areas,	once productive land, now stripped of vegetation and in need of resuscitation.

* Rapid and extensive *replanting of trees* for fuel: the bulk of humanity depends upon biomass fuels, mainly wood, for domestic energy needs but rural wood supplies are dwindling.
* Research and development on environmentally sound and economically viable alternatives to *nuclear energy* and on increasing its safety.
* Better *water management*, with the participation of local farmers.
* Use alternatives to chemical *fertilisers*, especially organic nutrients.
* Control of *pesticide* use and exports from industrialised countries and development of alternative methods of pest control.
* *Agroforestry*, with farming integrated with tree production for food, fodder, fuel and erosion control.
* *Fish farming* to increase food without decreasing wild fish stocks.

The Urban Challenge

* National *urban strategies* should involve both rural and urban planning in a complimentary rather than a contradictory way.
* *Local authorities* should be strengthened with political power, decision-making capacities and access to revenue.
* Increase the development of *secondary centres*, rather than of one or two major cities which otherwise attract all the revenue and migrants.
* Improve conditions for *low-quality settlements*.
* Make cheap loans available to *low-income groups*.

Continued. . .

Table 3.2 Objectives of the Brundtland Report (continued)

Energy
* Because of all the inherent problems involved in the increasing use of fossil fuels, there is no other realistic option but *renewable fuels*.
* Utilities should accept power from both large- and small-scale generators using renewable sources, in a *low-energy future*.

Industry
* *Industrial development* should be sustainable and not damaging to the environment.
* Industries should view *pollution* as a symptom of inefficiency in production and should recognise pollution as a cost in their production plans, with appropriate investment and government incentives.
* Governments should have *environmental goals* and enforce environmental laws, regulations, incentives and standards on industrial enterprises.

Species and Ecosystems
* *Conservation and development* should be linked by managing conservation schemes while maintaining development objectives.
* *National parks* should underpin development by protecting watersheds and soil and water regimes for agriculture.

Managing the Oceans, Antarctica and Space
* Oceans should be managed on an *international* basis for law enforcement, fisheries management and dumping, both directly and from rivers.
* Antarctica and space should be managed *internationally* for the common good.

Conflict and Environmental Degradation
* Definitions of *security* should include not only threats to national sovereignty but also environmental degradation and pre-emption of development options: unrest derives from environmental degradation as much as helping cause it.

Institutional and Legal Changes
* Globally connected environmental, development, security and economic issues should be dealt with from an *overall viewpoint*, not by fragmented institutions with narrow mandates.
* *Major international bodies* should be responsible and accountable for sustainable development policies.

interests are more important than more immediate interests before we can make progress.

We could now take any environmental problem we can think of and do a similar analysis. However, such a discussion would be anecdotal and specific to each problem. It would be better to have a more systematic recognition of agreement barriers which could be applied to any problem. Such a recognition does not mean that the barriers are inevitable, or necessarily operate in a particular sequence, but identifying them systematically will be useful because, if identified in the context of any one particular problem, they will provide a target for attention in the tackling of environmental problems in the future. First, can we define what we mean by an environmental problem more systematically?

What is an Environmental Problem?

There are at least two levels of approach to tackling the question of what constitutes an environmental problem, first, there is the general approach in terms of a situation which falls short of perceived goals, and second, the notion that specific conflicts of interest and values are involved.

Goal shortfall

On the first point, having discussed general goals of resource husbandry and sustainability earlier, we can say that an environmental problem can be seen as a situation where the resource base of the planet which supports life is damaged so as to decrease the quality of that resource, thus damaging the life which it supports, including our own. The resource base includes, soils, water, energy sources, food and shelter and the ability to support plant and animal life.

This general definition of an environmental problem involves the evaluation of the ways in which a situation affects the ability of the environment to support life. As far as people are concerned, this evaluation involves a situation which falls short of their goals and it can include both direct concerns about vested interests and livelihoods (personal goal shortfall) and a more altruistic concern about the intrinsic value of life on earth (environmental or ethical goal shortfall).

Conflicts of interest and values

The second point is that environmental problems are characterised by, and arise because of, a duality of attitudes. An environmental problem is thus one where *a situation exists which some people find damaging or unacceptable, while other people find it beneficial, acceptable or unimportant.*

The first group of people may feel that there is some personal disadvantage in a situation (if, for example, their soil is being washed away and their food resources lost (personal goal shortfall)); or that it is harmful to the environment and its ecosystems, even if there is no direct affect on them (like people in England being concerned about whaling in Antarctica (environmental or ethical goal shortfall)). The other group might feel that there is no goal shortfall or that a situation does not conflict with their goals or is irrelevant to them: they may benefit from the situation (they may be making money from it, or have at least a short-term benefit, say, from cash crops); or they may see no particular disadvantage in the situation (it does them no harm); or they may not see the point about environmental harm (they may not be concerned about the environment).

Thus there are questions both of self-interest and of values involved. Whether a situation is seen as a problem or not thus derives from whether environmental damage is perceived, how it affects, or does not affect, individuals or groups and how the environment is valued.

Do we Agree about the Problems?

We can now see that in order to tackle environmental problems, we can ask a systematic series of questions at specific stages:

1. Does a situation exist?
2. Is this situation a problem? If so, for whom?
3. Is this problem significant? If so, to whom?
4. What are the causes of the problem?
5. What is an appropriate solution – and appropriate for whom and for what goals?

We can describe what we mean by illustrating these stages with reference to the problem of acid rain. The first involves arguments about whether some situation or state actually occurs. Is there agreement that the rainfall is more acid now than it used to be? Are there reliable data on rainfall acidity which scientists accept and which other people also recognise?

The second involves arguments over whether acid rain is a problem. If it is agreed that rainfall is now more acid than it used to be, is there scientific and general agreement that it affects trees, buildings and health?

The third involves the extent and scope of the problem. If it is agreed that trees are dying, buildings are corroding and people's health is suffering, is it agreed whether the effects are widespread or local and whether many or few instances are involved?

The fourth involves identification of the sources of the problem. If it is agreed that the effects are widespread and significant, is it agreed that the causes actually involve acid rain and, if so, is it coming from power-station chimneys, vehicle exhausts or some other sources?

The fifth involves not only finding the target but also acting upon it. If it is agreed that both chimneys and vehicles are involved, do we agree that we have the technological means to tackle the sources? How much

Table 3.3 Problem specification: ozone depletion

Does the ozone hole exist?

Ozone depletion was first noticed in the Antarctic. The level here decreased from around 300 Dobson units* in the early 1960s to around 200 units in the early 1980s. 1987 levels dropped to only 15 Dobson units, a destruction of 5 per cent of the ozone. This is referred to as an 'ozone hole' and there is agreement that it exists.

Is there agreement that this represents a problem?

Enough satellite pictures of the ozone hole have been published in publicly available outlets for there to be wide awareness of the situation. This gave rise to increased awareness that the protective capacity of ozone to screen out harmful ultra-violet (UV) radiation is being reduced. UV is known to have a damaging effect on genetic material in living tissues, especially DNA, and can cause skin cancer. Some UV does penetrate the ozone screen naturally, but if the ozone is depleted the amount of UV light reaching the earth's surface will increase, with an increased potential for damage to life on earth.

Is there agreement that this problem is significant?

Publicity was given to the calculation that a 1 per cent depletion in ozone would result in an increase in skin cancers by 5 per cent. Friends of the Earth (FOE) cited American reports that an epidemic of skin cancers is likely with only a small increase in UV, with over 1 million extra cancers and 20,000 cases resulting in death. FOE also cited likely increases in eye disesases, such as cataracts, damage to agricultural crops and other plants and a worsening of smog pollution. It is agreed that the ozone hole represents a problem because there is a high correlation between skin cancer and UV and between UV and exposure to sunlight.

Although there is as yet no real evidence of increased skin cancer, the problem has received wide recognition and acceptance. This has formed a basis for research into the causes of ozone depletion, which has targeted the role of chlorofluorocarbons (CFCs) from aerosols and other sources in depleting the ozone layer, and thus also for action on the decreased use of CFCs.

* A Dobson unit is the thickness of ozone which would be present if all ozone dispersed in the atmosphere were compressed to sea level at normal temperature and pressure; in an atmospheric thickness of 8 km, the ozone in it is equivalent to 3 mm of pure ozone: 1 Dobson unit (DU) = 0.01 mm, so that 3 mm = 300 DU.

Source: Trudgill (1988) *Geography Review*

will it cost? Will it be socially and politically acceptable and will there be any other implications?

We can see that the resolution of a problem may be hindered by disagreements at many stages. According to the stage at which these stumbling blocks occur, we can designate them as follows:

Table 3.4 Problem specification: nitrate

What is the situation?

Farmers apply nitrate fertiliser to the land in order to increase crop growth. This has been encouraged by EEC agricultural policies but has recently come under criticism as contributing to food surpluses. Also not all of the nitrate is used by the crop. Some of it is washed through the soil by rainfall and is lost from the fields into streams.

Is this loss a problem?

Any loss of nitrate from fields represents an economic loss to the farmers, in terms both of loss of expensive fertiliser and of reduced crop yields. Nitrate can act as a fertiliser in streams and lakes, causing rapid aquatic plant growth and other undesirable ecological changes. A high nitrate concentration in drinking water can be damaging to human health.

Is the problem significant?

It can be argued that fertiliser loss can be seen as an inevitable consequence of a productive agriculture. The concerns are over the need for such production, human health and environmental effects. There is some controversy over the precise links with human health: while the links between high nitrate levels in drinking water and methaemoglobinaemia ('blue babies') are established, there is less certainty over the suggested link between nitrate and stomach cancer. There is also debate over the extent of freshwater ecological changes and the role of nitrate in causing them relative to other nutrients, especially phosphate. There is some dispute as to appropriate action and whether the emphasis should be on agricultural policy, decreased use of fertilisers and/or water treatment.

Source: as Table 3.3

1. Situation uncertainty.
2. Problem uncertainty.
3. Significance uncertainty.
4. Causal uncertainty.
5. Resolution uncertainty.

All these uncertainties have to be resolved before a problem can be successfully tackled. Here we shall tackle the first three, which are concerned with whether there is agreement over a problem or not. If there is agreement, we can then proceed to the next barrier, that of knowledge limitations about causes (causal uncertainty, see Chapter 4) and the subsequent ones of the economic, social and political barriers involved in the implementation of a solution (resolution uncertainty, see Chapter 6).

Generally speaking, it is the task of those who see a situation as a problem to persuade those who do not that the problem exists and should

Table 3.5 Problem specification: lead

What is the situation?

Lead is present in the environment and can be ingested by humans. Lead in the environment can be increased by human activity, including adding lead to petrol.

Is this a problem?

The effects of lead on human health include acute poisoning due to rapid uptake, or accumulation to chronic levels by the ingestion of smaller doses over time. Lead can disrupt metabolic pathways and can also affect the central nervous system and the brain. Significant mental retardation in young children is thought to be caused by high levels of lead ingestion.

Is this problem significant?

There are documented cases of undesirable levels of lead in human tissue. Lead in the environment is recognised as a problem since its toxic effects are well known. The UK Royal Commission on Environmental Pollution (RCEP, 1983) concluded that 'it is imprudent to continue adding such a persistent and toxic pollutant as lead to the environment'. UK action on lead now includes tax incentives for the use of unleaded petrol.

Source: as Table 3.3

be resolved. This involves identifying those with the means to tackle the problem and persuading them to act, whether they be governments, other organisations or individuals. We can thus see that the existence of a problem and the motivation to find a solution come from the same people – those who see situation as a problem. These people then have a threefold task:

1. *Demonstrating that a situation exists* (situation specification).
2. *Demonstrating that this situation is a problem* (problem specification).
3. *Demonstrating that this problem is significant* (significance specification).

In these three specifications, *evidence* is crucial. Scientific research is involved in situation specification and with establishing, beyond reasonable doubt if possible, *what evidence there is that a situation exists*.

Then we can proceed to the question of evidence that this situation is a problem and that the problem is significant. *Persuasion* is important in terms of presenting the evidence to those who may have it in their power to alter the situation.

There will then be questions of *acceptance* or *rejection* of the evidence at each stage. Then, even if the evidence is accepted, there may be an attitude of problem *denial*. Denial can take many forms, often in relation to the perceptions and values of groups and individuals according to their beliefs, motivations and vested interests. The directness of any effect on people is also important, as is the scope of the problem – whether it be local, regional or global – and also how the problem is seen relative to other problems.

Resolving situation uncertainty and problem uncertainty forms part of *problem specification*, where the nature, dimensions, causes and effects of the problem are detailed. This involves agreeing what the problem actually is and how it is manifested. There will, of course, be different versions of, and disagreements about, problem specification, so we shall return to this topic later when we have discussed other specific agreement barriers. However, unless a problem can be clearly specified there is little chance of proceeding to finding a solution or *problem resolution*.

This also raises a further question of what a solution actually is. Does it resolve completely all aspects of the perceived problem? Does it just cope with the more evident problems (for example, disposal of nuclear waste) or does it tackle the problem more fundamentally (for example, asking whether we need nuclear power at all or should be using alternative forms of energy – or, more fundamentally, whether we need such high levels of energy consumption).

In addition, does the solution to one problem lead to further problems? For example, promoting nuclear power to reduce carbon dioxide emissions and lessen the greenhouse effect may lead to further nuclear waste disposal problems. We can now summarise the sequence of situation and problem recognition (Figure 3.2), and then discuss situations, problems and their significance in more detail.

Situation uncertainty

In *situation uncertainty*, there is lack of agreement over the evidence that a situation exists at all. Some people at least believe that a situation exists, which we can call *situation awareness*. But the arguments stem either from a lack of evidence, or from different interpretations of the available evidence about the existence of a situation.

This can usually be resolved by further survey and measurement, that is, by gaining further evidence. For example, some ornithologists might argue that numbers of a particular bird species have declined in a particular area but others could attempt to refute this on the basis of their own observations. Here, detailed bird counts could resolve the issue but the argument may well stem, as it often does with changes over time, from the lack of accurate estimates of previous numbers. We can tell what is happening now by measurement, spurred on by the perception of a possible current problem, but the arguments may well then stem from a lack of previous measurements with which to compare the current ones. So it is difficult, in fact, to tell whether bird numbers have declined or not. This, then, remains a case of situation uncertainty – unless further data can be gained about changes over time to clarify the situation.

Figure 3.2 The stages leading up to the recognition of an environmental problem. Situation uncertainty, situation refutation and problem denial (shaded) represent barriers to progression and may have to be overcome before a problem is recognised.

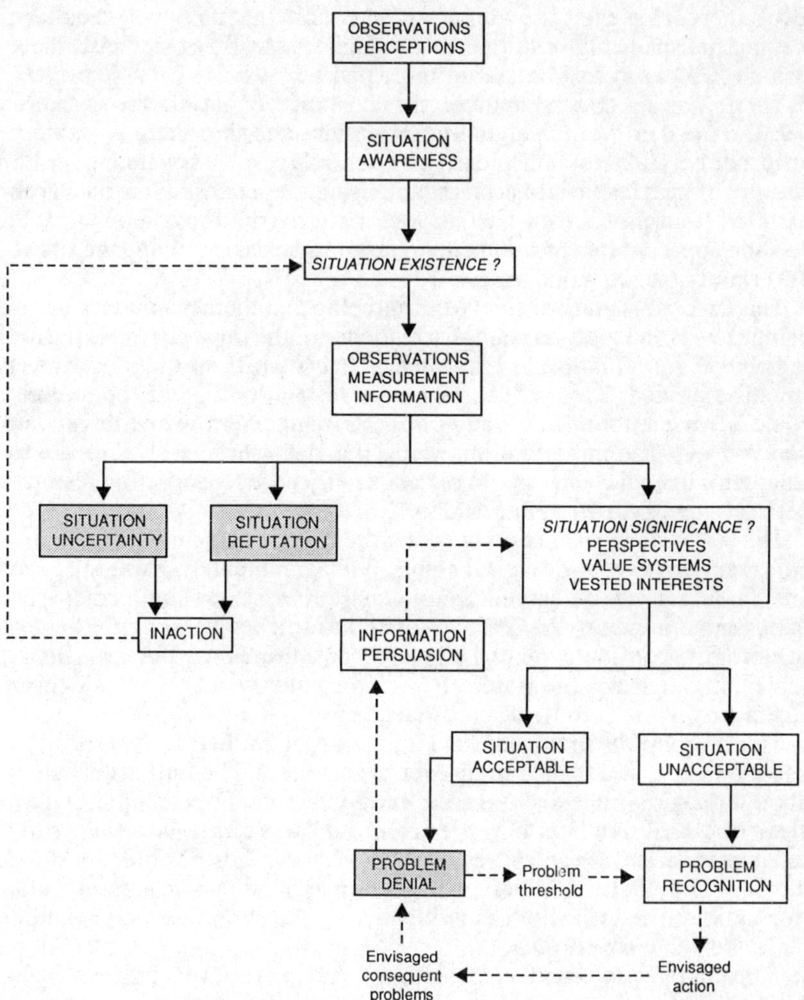

Situation uncertainty often involves arguments over patterns and trends, but it is not, at this stage, concerned with cause and effect. A further actual example of whether a situation existed or not is provided by the study of leukaemia in the vicinity of Sellafield nuclear power plant in Cumbria, England. The argument here was over whether a pattern of higher leukaemia levels existed round the plant or not. When evidence was produced to show that levels were higher immediately around the plant than they were in the region as a whole, it was argued that this established a situation of local high levels there. However, the counterargument ran that this level of leukaemia was not unusually high and that similar high levels also existed elsewhere in Britain, well away from nuclear power plants.

There was disagreement over the existence of an effect, or pattern, because the data were open to interpretation, and thus there was situation uncertainty. This situation uncertainty was only resolved by taking the other clusters of high levels into account and using them to establish background patterns of levels against which the local pattern could be compared. It then became apparent that an anomalous cluster did exist, resolving the situation uncertainty (see Macmillan, 1988).

This exercise is quite distinct from agreeing that there is a pattern or effect of high levels and then searching for evidence of the causes because the initial search was for a pattern of leukaemia clusters which would identify that a situation existed. This is at a stage of investigation before the inferences could be made about cause and effect. Disagreement over causes (causal uncertainty) is an important knowledge barrier which we shall return to in Chapter 4 but which we should discuss briefly here to clarify the distinction between it and situation uncertainty.

There is a clear distinction between the lack of agreement over whether *effects* exist or not, as discussed above, and agreement over what the *causes* are, once it has been agreed that a situation exists. In the former we are discussing arguments over effects – whether some state or condition exists or not and, if it does, then whether this constitutes a problem. This is an argument about desired states of the environment and about evidence for changes away from these desired states.

This is quite distinct from having already identified and agreed that a situation exists and then arguing over the causes and limitations of evidence about linkages, processes and contributary factors. For example, it may be clear that bird numbers have declined, and there may be yearly surveys to support this, but the causes could be a hard, frosty winter, pesticides, increase in predator numbers, persecution by man and/or a purely natural fluctuation. The difficulty lies in identifying the causative factors and may be termed *causal uncertainty*.

Thus, in the case of leukaemia clusters, having resolved arguments about their existence, the arguments move on from ones of situation uncertainty to become ones of causal uncertainty and whether nuclear plants or other causes are involved in producing the clusters.

Situation uncertainty, then, stems largely from inadequate information about states, conditions or patterns and leads to inaction. It can be resolved when perceptions and observations of what might be a trend or pattern act as a spur to greater information gathering and analysis. This can lead to *situation refutation* when it is clear that there is no situation which could constitute a problem; continued situation uncertainty occurs if the patterns are still debatable; and *situation recognition* occurs if the patterns become clear. The first two obviously lead to inaction but the last, situation recognition, can lead to consideration of whether this situation constitutes a problem or not.

Problem uncertainty

Whether or not a situation constitutes a problem is a matter of *problem uncertainty* in relation to situation significance. This again includes a duality in that some people involved recognise a situation as unacceptable and as a problem, which we call *problem recognition*, while others deny that the situation constitutes a problem, which we call *problem denial*.

In problem denial there may be a clear agreement that some state or situation exists, with clear evidence of an effect, but at least some people involved may deny that it is a problem. There is thus a question of groups with contrasting viewpoints – one says that some clearly recognised state, condition or action is a problem, the other says that it is not. For example, a pond may be clearly seen to be covered with green scum, a situation which nobody could fail to recognise; some people could see this as a problem, requiring a solution, others may see it as no problem at all.

There is also a question of degree in this – there may be a recognised problem, but it may not be thought to be severe enough to consider doing anything about it. This is an issue of *problem thresholds* which could turn problem denial into problem recognition.

A barrier to problem-solving obviously does not occur if problem recognition is universal, but only if it is partial and coupled with problem denial from other quarters. The analysis then becomes one of whether recognition and denial is from those affected, those causing the problem and/or those who can do anything about it. This is obviously at the heart of many problems. Clearly problem denial cannot be universal as the problem would not have been posed as such in the first place; equally, if recognition is universal, then we will rapidly move towards resolution. Problems arise, almost by definition, from problem uncertainty and where both recognition and denial are found, classically with recognition from those affected and denial from those causing it and where the progress of resolution is related to the attitude of those who can do something about it.

Since problem denial is a matter of perception of significance of phenomena, this can only be overcome by persuasion, altering people's value system, and/or demonstration of the detrimental effects of an evident state (for example, the green scum is harming wild animals or plants, the wildlife thus affected matters to us . . . and so on). However, in order to overcome problem denial, it is important to understand the specific reasons why such a reaction occurs.

Perspectives

Because a problem may be denied by groups possessing different perspectives, value systems and vested interests from those who adopt problem recognition, problem denial can often be seen as a matter of *problem perspectives*. Here, as we said earlier, we can see that problem recognition is a matter of assessing whether a situation affects people adversely and/or clashes with their value systems.

An additional point about perspectives is that action taken to solve a problem seen by one person or group can become the inception of another's problem – and which is not agreed to be a problem by the first party. This can be termed *consequent problem*. There is agreement that the first problem existed but a denial, among the first party, that the consequent problem exists. Alternatively, recognition of an unacceptable consequent problem can be cited as a reason in support of the denial of an initial problem.

A fundamental consideration in this is that each person, or group, has its own sphere of reference. Action is taken within this sphere of reference, and other factors are not necessarily considered. Thus, action may be taken to have a particular effect and the success of the action may then be measured only in terms of achieving that effect; other ramifications and side-effects are not necessarily considered.

The natures of problem denial, thresholds, perspectives and consequent problems can be illustrated with reference to agricultural hedge removal. Farmers may remove hedges in order to increase field size to a more efficient level. This, from the perspective of the farmers, is not a problem, indeed it is seen as a benefit. However, from the perspective of conservationists, this may represent a problem if the hedge has conservation value in terms of wild flowers, birds and insects or if the hedge has a historical conservation value because it is an old woodland boundary. This problem can be denied by farmers, who could argue that each kilometre of hedge removed represents a gain of 0.88 hectares of land, thus increasing the land available for production and farm viability. To the farmers, it is the conservationists who are making what was seen as a simple management action into a problem. If farmers are sympathetic to a conservation viewpoint, they may well not remove the hedge, having been appaised of its value. If they are not, then they they may simply remove the hedge, disagreeing that the consequent problem of conservation loss existed or mattered. Thus, there would be no agreement that a problem existed. A solution to the problem of hedge removal would thus not necessarily be found because only some of the people involved thought it was a problem according to their perspectives. The farmers could, however, see the situation as a problem if their perspectives were altered and hedge removal led to an increase in soil erosion by wind, the sheltering effect of the hedge having been removed, and there was a loss in productivity and economic viability as a result.

In the UK in recent years, it was only when hedge removal became widespread that a problem threshold was reached and public opinion swung round to identifying and tackling the problem, especially by trying to change the value system of people who removed hedges: thus Oliver Rackham (1986), writing on the history of the British countryside, felt that hedge removal can represent 'a loss of beauty . . . historic vegetation . . . and a loss of meaning'. Rackham also records how perspectives have changed: it is a 'fallacy that the destruction is necessary. People still rehearse the arguments, some of them quite good ones (bigger fields, more land needed, etc.), without realizing that times have changed and that these are no longer good arguments for destroying such . . . [old] hedges'. Thus, initial problem denial by the farmer was followed by a tackling of the problem, partly by a recognition of a common interest in retaining hedges to prevent soil erosion and to preserve their conservation value but mainly because of the different perspective put on it, as in so many cases, by changing economics, which has made it less imperative to produce more in the late 1980s (notwithstanding that cynics observed that there were few hedges left to remove!). It is clear also that consequent problems might have been denied by the farmer when they did not affect the farm or were not seen as significant but also that a consequent problem of soil erosion, which affected the farmer's livelihood, could alter the perspective of the farmer and remove the problem denial.

Summary of Situation and Problem Uncertainty

We can see that there has been an interaction between problem denial, problem thresholds, changing perspectives and information about consequences which have influenced the degrees of agreement over this problem and the ways in which it has evolved over time. It is also worth noting that while there was some measure of agreement between those involved, the course of the problem through time was perhaps overtaken by events and more influenced by external economic factors than by the degree of agreement. As we said in Chapter 2, the AKTESP barriers are not rigid, but a focus for attention, and thus we may learn that while disagreement may be a barrier to finding a solution, agreement is not a necessary prerequisite for solution if there are other, external, events which have a stronger influence in rendering a problem-causing activity no longer defensible.

The key points are:

1. Awareness of possible situations may exist and further investigation may lead to a state of situation refutation, situation uncertainty or situation recognition.
2. With situation recognition, clearly visible states may exist, but these can be seen as not significant and thus denied as problem states (problem denial).

3. Denial may be a matter of insufficient impact of the problem (problem threshold).
4. Denial often varies with viewpoint (problem perspective).
5. Denial may stem from consequent problems which follow remedial actions, but consequent problems may also alter problem perspectives.

The systematic stages (as illustrated earlier in Figure 3.2 on p.31) are:

1. Perception and observation give rise to situation awareness.
2. This can be refused or recognised or remain uncertain through further observation, measurement and information.
3. Situation recognition can be met with problem recognition or denial through evaluations of situation significance, with an acceptable situation leading to problem denial and an unacceptable one leading to problem recognition.
4. Denial can change to recognition through thresholds of degree or extent or changed perspectives, often from external forces.
5. Problem recognition can lead to envisaged action but envisaged consequent problems can lead to further denial or, via changed perspectives, further problem recognition.

We have seen so far that agreement barriers can involve disagreement over effects, usually as a result of inadequate information (situation uncertainty); and disagreement about the significance of situations, brought about largely by different perspectives (problem denial). If we overcome these barriers, we have both situation recognition and problem recognition. Problem recognition does not necessarily then lead automatically to action – there are other barriers which then may arise. Problem recognition is a prerequisite of action – just as situation recognition is a prerequisite of problem recognition – but neither is sufficient in itself for progress to be made to the next stage. This is because there is an intervening stage which involves assessments of the *significance* of the problem – a stage which can lead either to problem acceptance or to problem rejection, despite the recognition of the existence of the problem.

Problem significance

In problem significance it may be agreed and recognised that a problem exists (problem recognition), but it may not be seen as significant enough to bother with for some reason. So the problem may be recognised but rejected, and we can talk of *problem rejection*. The reasons for not bothering may involve thresholds, as mentioned earlier, or the directness of the effect or its significance in relation to other considerations. Thus there are two important dimensions of problem significance and acceptance to consider: the scope of the problem, in terms of the immediacy and scale of its effects; and the dimensions of the problem relative to other problems in people's lives.

PROBLEM IMMEDIACY

Problem rejection can have a purely *utilitarian*, or functional dimension, where the effects are seen solely in terms of the direct effects of a problem on the individual or group under consideration. Thus, an English schoolchild might say: 'I know that the destruction of the tropical rainforest is a problem, but how does affect me? It is a long way away, so why should I worry about it? Aren't there more immediate problems I should be concerned with in my own backyard?' A farmer might say: 'I know that using nitrogen fertiliser causes the problem of eutrophication in streams and lakes, but I can't produce good crops without it and so I am going to carry on using it or I shall go out of business.' These are classic examples of problem rejection, despite recognition. The first is a matter of value systems and the second is an understandable one of economic pressures, though not without an underlying value system that accepts that pressure as paramount. We should also note that both these attitudes might be inherent in original problem denial, but this would be unusual in these cases because information about tropical rainforests and the effects of fertilisers is widely publicised.

Alternatively, there could be a reaction of *problem acceptance*, where the problem is both recognised as existing and accepted as important. Here, as with problem recognition, there may be an acceptance because the problem affects the individual *adversely* and *directly* or, for less immediate problems, there may be a more *altruistic*, *idealistic* value system existing which feels that any problem, anywhere, should be tackled, not because of a direct effect on the person concerned, but because of a wider recognition of the intrinsic value of the environment. This is more a moral question of environmental ethics and shows a wider awareness of the planet as a whole, the extent of planetary interrelations and the intrinsic qualities of the ecosystem.

Clearly, an attitude which is more likely to lead to problem rejection is one which sees immediate self-interest as the most important criterion, and it could therefore be termed *parochial problem rejection*. Overcoming this attitude can be difficult but it can be attempted in one of two ways. The first is to accept the inherent attitude and show that far-off places do have an effect on the parochially minded individual. Here the arguments often rehearsed for the acceptance of rainforest destruction as a problem include the ways in which evaporation and photosynthesis in the rainforest affect world rainfall and carbon dioxide levels, which could affect us all through world climate mechanisms and which should therefore be of concern to everyone. In addition, there are more direct arguments such as the point that a quarter of pharmaceutical products have their origin in tropical rainforests. The other is to educate beyond this parochial attitude, which is more difficult. Basically, the task is to promote feelings for the rights of other species and how we, as the dominant species on the planet, have a responsibility to maintain the integrity of other ecosystems. The essential point is that the planet is our backyard. Television has done a lot in this direction by screening pictures of endearing, interesting or awesome animals and plants which can evoke a sense of wonder, stewardship and responsibility in the viewer. A qualification here, though, is that if the programmes end with a message of gloom and destruction, rather than promoting a caring attitude or galvanising the viewer into action, they may induce negative feelings of helplessness, of things being beyond our control. This can have the reverse effect and make people retract more into parochial issues where they can have some influence. It is thus important for these programmes to show positive steps which have been, and can be, taken to safeguard the ecosystems – and how the individual can help. This could be, for example, by the decreased use of tropical hardwoods in European countries, though this, in itself, can be complicated because the exploitation of wood relates to the needs of indigenous people to make a living and so alternative forms of sustainable, non-ecologically damaging forestry and other ways of making a living must also be indicated.

Tackling the more economically motivated rejection is more difficult, as in the case of the farmer using nitrate even though he or she was aware of the environmental consequences. Here, it is a question either of working within the current economic system, where compensation would be appropriate if a loss were incurred by tackling the problem, or of changing the underlying value system that gives rise to this economic motivation. This could be by an overall approach to agricultural policy or by pointing out the relative merits of alternative approaches, including both their economic and environmental merits.

We can see, then, that problem rejection is not a matter of whether the problem exists or not, but a matter of recognition that a problem exists but that it is beyond the scope or inclination of the individual to do anything about it, either from a feeling of inability to influence it or because it is seen as less significant than some other more immediate problem. Thus, we can insert further barriers, which have to be overcome, between problem recognition and action, those of problem significance involving aspects of scope and immediacy.

PROBLEM SCALE

This dimension of problem significance is concerned with how many people, species or resources and/or how wide an area a problem affects. Problem rejection can arise if the problem is seen as too overwhelming or global for individual action to have any impact but equally also because it may be perceived that not many people, species or resources or only a small area are affected. In the latter case, a problem may be recognised but not accepted as one where action was necessary because of the limited scale of the problem. There would be greater agreement and acceptance that a problem was significant if it could be shown that the problem had wide scope, and that it affected a great number of people, a great number of species, a widely used resource or a large area. Values are also important here: some species or environments are valued more than others and one consideration is how rare or common an affected species is. Thus, there is more likely to be agreement if a valued, rare species or environments of national or international importance are involved.

Conversely, problems with wide scope may be easier to recognise and accept but more difficult to tackle. Thus, if the whole of the North Sea to the Mediterranean is affected by pollution, this would have very wide recognition and acceptance but the points at which it would need tackling are many, making the problem difficult to solve. This can be termed *problem complexity*, and it may, in itself, lead to subsequent problem rejection, and is an important factor in the reluctance to take on water- and air-pollution problems involving many sources.

Problem relativity

A further consideration in problem significance and acceptance is one of problem relativity. Here, the question is how important the environmental problem is relative to other problems in people's lives. A classic clash is between unemployment and conservation. There is an oft-rehearsed argument that environmental issues must take second place to employment and people's livelihoods. In the long term one may argue that the points converge and that a good environment is part of a thriving community which promotes good job prospects, but often, in the short term, there is disagreement, and we see, for example, arguments over the building of a reservoir for industry and employment at the sacrifice of rare plants or conservation value. Certainly, if a farmer is struggling to make a living, then he or she may take actions to improve productivity which may not be environmentally desirable, such as ploughing up marginal land. The greater problem is seen as one of livelihood rather than of environment and conservation.

Problem Significance: Summary

It can be seen that the barriers between problem recognition and acceptance involve assessments of the significance of the problem. In terms of *problem scope* it may be *less immediate* or *too overwhelming* or *too small in scale*. It may also be *small relative to other problems*.

All this reduces to a question of the *significance* placed on the problem which is at a stage beyond that of initial problem recognition and involves subsequent problem rejection or problem acceptance. Once accepted, the problem may be subsequently rejected because of *problem complexity*.

We can therefore now redraw the lower part of Figure 3.2 (p.31) in a more realistic way (Figure 3.3). Here, factors like immediacy, scale and relativity lead to an assessment of problem significance and problem acceptance or rejection, even though the problem's existence has now been recognised. Problem complexity may also lead to problem rejection subsequent to acceptance.

Figure 3.3 The stages leading from problem recognition to specification. Problems may be rejected (shaded) if they are not seen as significant or are seen as too complex. These rejections have to be overcome before the problem is accepted.

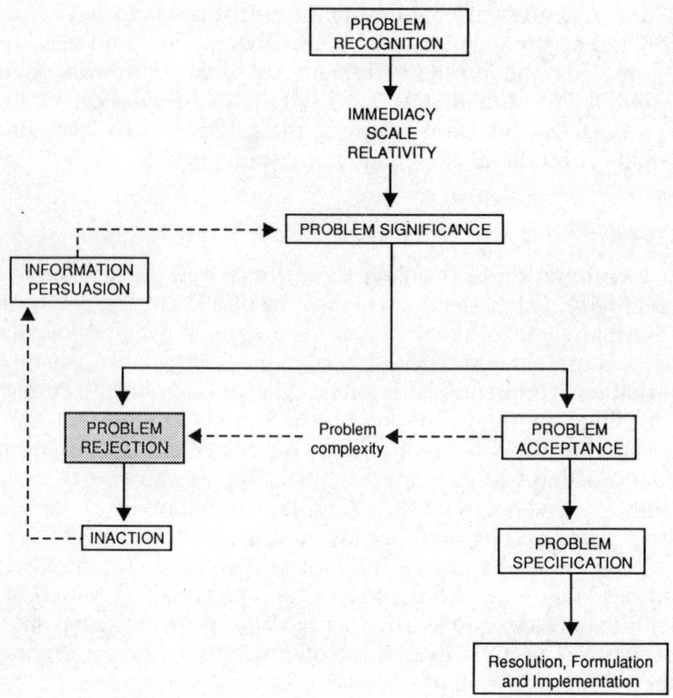

We have now established that agreement barriers can involve situation uncertainty, situation significance and problem denial. We have also established that even where problem recognition occurs, agreement over problem significance varies and forms a further barrier of problem rejection. We should now confirm what these barriers may mean in relation to what actually constitutes an environmental problem.

Redefining an Environmental Problem

We began by suggesting that an environmental problem could be seen, in general terms, as *a situation where the resource base of the planet which supports life is damaged in such a way as to decrease the quality of the resource, thus damaging the life which it supports*.

Now, having spent some time discussing the barriers of agreement as to what is a problem, it is apparent that we can confirm a perception-centred viewpoint whereby an environmental problem can be defined as *a situation which some people, but not others, actually see as a environmental problem*.

This duality of views is an important point. Problems are defined by our concepts of problems, rather than by any more abstract or objective assessments. This means that we should qualify our first definition, adding *that only some people recognise the situation as a problem, whether to themselves, or to the wider environment beyond their immediate surroundings*.

The 'some people see' aspect implies that a degree of agreement exists but that it is only partial. We can thus see that a problem exists only at certain stages of Figures 3.2 and 3.3, and that is beyond the levels of situation recognition. This implies that an environmental problem involves a *recognised situation which some people, at least, find unacceptable (problem recognition) but others do not recognise (problem denial)*. Before this stage, the problem does not exist, as it is not formulated as such, but is only a situation. After this, remedial action is possible and one has moved on to further stages involving acceptance or rejection.

The important level of acceptance is one where decision-makers are involved, whether it be individuals involved directly, societies, pressure groups, landowners, local, regional or national governments or international organisations. This is the level of agreement at which a problem may cease to be a problem because something is done to tackle it.

So when we ask when an environmental problem is a problem, we can suggest that it is simply so when people disagree about the significance of a situation. And when we ask why we do not solve more problems, the answer lies, first, in a greater understanding of this situation significance, and especially of the implications of the situation, and second, in understanding and working with the varying perspectives on situations which exist.

This means that an important step in problem resolution lies in a general *problem specification*. What exactly is the problem? What are its dimensions? What are its effects? What do people disagree about? Is it the degree of recognition or the significance of the problem? If there is problem acceptance, does rejection arise from problem complexity?

A crucial barrier thus involves agreement as to what a problem actually is. Thus we have to agree on the dimensions of the problem once we have agreed that one exists. This involves components of situation recognition, problem recognition and problem acceptance. Here, we have to agree not only on the causes and effects but also specify precisely the ways in which the problem manifests itself before we can move to a solution.

Thus, it is not just a case of crying 'water pollution' but of specifying what pollutants are involved, what their sources are, and what it affects in terms of, for example, indices of water quality such as acidity, biological oxygen demand and turbidity, and then to assess what species of plant and animal are affected and in what way. Is the effect toxic or sub-lethal but damaging, does it affect species reproduction, behaviour, and so on? Is the effect very local or more widespread? Does it ramify through the system to affect other species?

This also means that there is a need for information about the effects of the problem and about attitudes to it. Resolution involves evaluation of the possible effects of varying courses of action or inaction and a stimulation of the value system so that those involved can overcome, or at least critically examine, any problem denial or problem rejection. Hidden in this are the economic, social and political factors which are especially important in leading to problem rejection – other factors concerned with livelihood, social customs and political power often lead to the relegation of an environmental problem to a subordinate consideration. This also brings up the question of whether environmental problems are more important than economic, social or political problems.

We are, however, perhaps clear enough now to say that an environmental problem is not only one which *detracts from the resource base of the planet and its life-support system* but also one where there is *a situation which some people see as a detraction from the resource base and its life-support system but where others deny that such a detraction exists*, or even where *there is general acceptance of a problem but it is seen as too complex, unweildy or difficult to do anything about it*.

Thus not only problem recognition and acceptance but also problem denial and rejection are inherent in the specification of a problem. Disagreement is thus a cause inherent in problems and also a barrier to solving them. This realisation has got to be at the heart of environmental problem-solving because, when we ask why we do not solve more environmental problems, the answer must lie in examining, and dealing with, the reasons for denial and rejection.

We can conclude with a summary definition. *An environmental problem exists if there is a situation where the resource base of the planet which supports life is damaged in such a way as to decreases the quality of the resource, thus damaging the life which it supports, and which involves disagreement in that only some people involved recognise that the situation is unacceptable while others deny its significance, or where there is a situation which most people recognise as unacceptable but where progress to a resolution is impeded by some other barrier*. In other (and fewer) words, *an environmental problem is a resource- and life-damaging situation which is not universally recognised or is difficult to improve*.

Agreement Barriers: A Summary

Lack of agreement can constitute a major barrier to a better environment. This lack of agreement can involve:

1. The scope of solutions – fundamental or limited?
2. Goals, including the differences between environmental and non-environmental goals, and between personal and wider goals.
3. How to translate goals into action for specific problems.

Figure 3.4 Summary of the stages between the awareness of a situation and the formulation of solution. Evaluation points are critical questions which can lead to inaction (shaded) or progression.

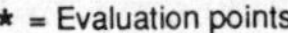

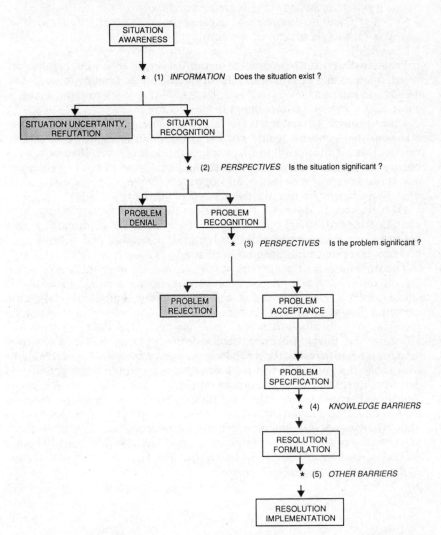

We therefore need more discussion, and more accord on environmental goals – especially about the reorientation of non-environmental goals and about how far we can go with the scope of solutions, with a wider acceptance that fundamental solutions and goals are eventually more effective than a series of limited, adaptive ones.

For specific problems, the lack of agreement can be about:

1. Whether or not a situation exists (situation uncertainty).
2. If a situation is agreed to exist (situation recognition), what the significance of the situation is (situation significance), and whether a problem exists or not (problem denial).
3. If a problem is recognised as existing (problem recognition), whether it is seen as significant or not (problem rejection).

Problem denial and rejection are matters of *perspective, value systems* and *vested interests* and can therefore be tackled by understanding these factors and by information about effects of actions, education of awareness and, as a last resort, by legal enforcement in an effective manner.

Disagreement at some level is inherent in environmental problems, otherwise the problem would not exist, but even in cases of agreement (problem recognition and problem acceptance), there may then be further barriers to progress. Here, the countering force involves not disagreement but causal uncertainty, a lack of appropriate *technology or economic, social or political factors*, as discussed in Chapters 5 and 6.

Problem specification is a vital consideration at many stages because it can affect denial, rejection and significance reactions at an earlier stage of problem agreement and also subsequent reactions and actions once problem acceptance has been reached at a later stage.

The stages involved in agreement barriers are summarised in Figure 3.4. and involve disagreements over *situation existence and significance* and about *problem existence and significance*. Disagreement over situation existence forms a barrier between situation awareness and situation recognition at evaluation point (1). Disagreements over situation significance and thus problem existence form a barrier between situation recognition and problem recognition at evaluation point (2). Disagreements over problem significance forms a barrier between problem recognition and problem acceptance at evaluation point (3).

If these barriers do not exist, or if they do and can be overcome by more *evidence* and *persuasion*, then the problem is accepted and the field of endeavour moves into one of resolution formulation and implementation. Here, many other barriers can become apparent, the first being whether we know enough to be able to tackle the problem, and this is discussed in the next chapter.

Chapter 4

Knowledge Barriers

Do we know enough to be able to tackle environmental problems? Can we identify causes of problems or pinpoint sources? Do we have enough knowledge to be able to identify possible effective solutions? These questions essentially involve the activities and endeavours of environmental scientists and knowledge of the physics, chemistry and biology of the environment as well as of the complexities of interactions in natural systems. Again, we can illustrate some of the barriers by reference to the three examples we used in Chapter 3.

Let us first consider ozone depletion. Initially the links between man-made pollutants and ozone depletion were not clear. The fundamental processes involving ozone and ultraviolet radiation were known, but scientists were uncertain about the specific action of man-made pollutants on ozone. However, this uncertainty was rapidly being overcome by the mid-1980s. Since we cannot easily watch chemical reactions happening in the upper atmosphere, the evidence for the causal links involved identifying possible chemical processes and then finding the relevant chemical reactants and products in the upper atmosphere. Scientific research thus involved remote sensing, upper air sampling and spectrophotometer work from the ground. Such work received wide publicity, not only in the scientific press but also in the popular press.

We already knew that ozone can be both created and destroyed in the upper atmosphere. It is formed in the upper atmosphere by a chain of events which starts with the splitting of oxygen gas (O_2) under the action of UV radiation. This splitting produces single oxygen atoms (O), referred to as monatomic oxygen. Further oxygen gas then combines with monatomic oxygen by collision to form ozone (O_3). Ozone can be broken down again into oxygen gas by collisions with monatomic oxygen or by the action of UV. During this process of creation and destruction, ozone absorbs all UV radiation of wavelengths less than 0.29 μm, which decreases its penetration earthwards.

However, what became established was that this naturally balanced cycle can be disturbed because ozone can also be broken down by combination with atmospheric pollutants, especially chlorine (Ko *et al.*, 1987). The ozone

Figure 4.1 Mechanism for the depletion of ozone. Chlorofluorocarbons (CFCs) produce chlorine in ultraviolet light (UV) and then interact with ozone (O_3), breaking it down, leaving chlorine intact for further ozone destruction.

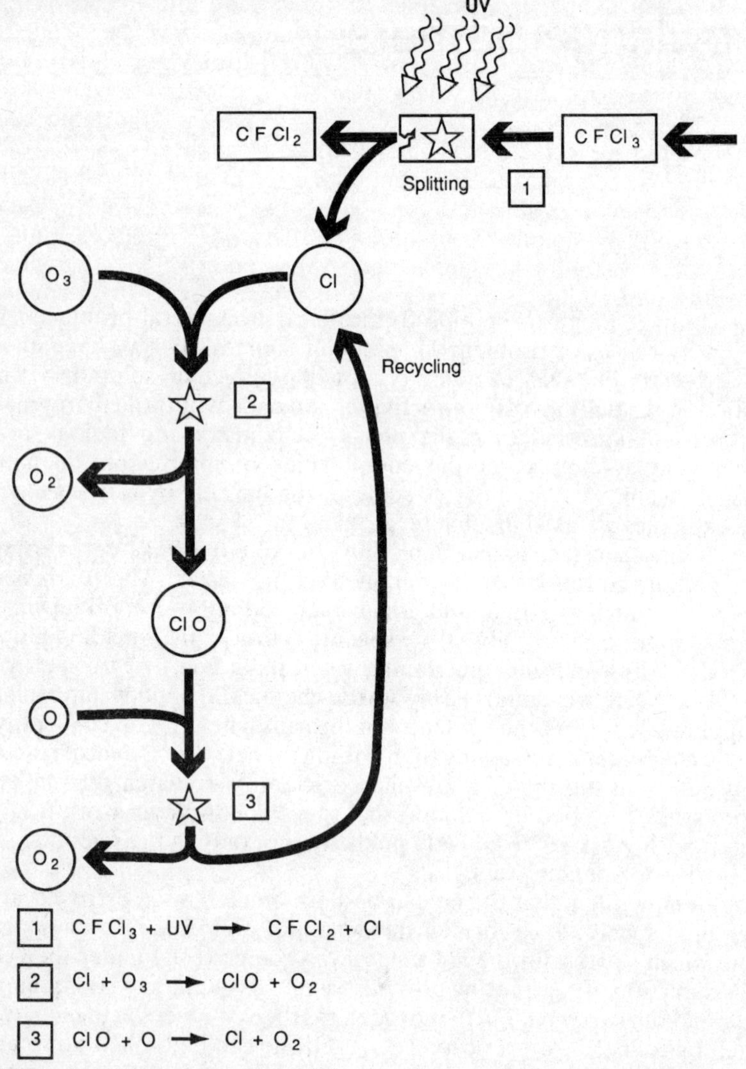

combines with the pollutant and, if monatomic oxygen is also present, the pollutant is recycled intact to destroy more ozone as described by Farman (1987) and illustrated in Figure 4.1.

Chlorofluorocarbons (CFCs) produce chlorofluoromethane gases, commonly CF_2Cl_2 (also called F-12) and $CFC1_3$ (F-11). UV radiation acts on them to produce chlorine. The chlorine sinks into the ozone layer, breaking down ozone. This produces further chlorine. These reactions effectively remove ozone from the cycle of creation and destruction without using up chlorine. Thus, once present the chlorine is liable to have a long-term damaging effect.

Scientists at the British Antarctic Survey station at Halley Bay detected an abundance of chlorine at 18 km in the atmosphere. It is possible that this could have a volcanic source, but they have also recorded the presence of fluorine, a substance which only has man-made sources, confirming the presence of anthropogenic pollutants in the upper atmosphere.

Man-made polluting substances involved in damaging the ozone screen are now accepted to be mainly chlorine from CFCs. These are used as aerosol propellants, in refrigerators as coolants and in foam blowing in the manufacture of foam furniture, some fast-food cartons and insulating materials. Levels of CFCs in the upper atmosphere over the Antarctic have been monitored since 1970 and have increased since that time.

Thus, knowledge barriers involved were present initially but uncertainty over causes was responded to by the scientific community which argued by evidence of association (pollutant presence and ozone depletion) and by mechanism postulation to decrease mechanism uncertainty. It is probable that a widespread acceptance of the problem led to such a large effort on the part of the scientific community on its causes.

Having argued that man-made pollutants were involved, the proposed management action clearly involved reducing CFC usage. Once this was proposed, however, an interesting stage was reached as the argument grew that we should wait for more hard evidence about the mechanism of ozone destruction and the links with CFCs. This arose because of initial uncertainty over causes. Rather than waiting for more research and evidence, Friends of the Earth took the view that the evidence was already strong enough, and called for immediate action to reduce production of CFCs, having already published a list of some 2000 CFC-free aerosols including polishes, deodorants, room fresheners and cleansing fluids. Technological barriers were not involved here because, as alternatives, there are simpler pressure devices which are hand-pumped and other propellant gases which can be used, such as butane and pentane. Calls for action thus then moved into the economic, social and political arena.

Let us now move on to consider nitrate. Nitrate is an important nutrient for freshwater and terrestrial plants alike. Thus, when nitrate is leached into streams and lakes from either fertiliser or natural sources, it acts as a nutrient for both the larger water plants and the microscopic algae. These are then encouraged to grow by the extra input of nutrients. This nutrient enrichment is termed *eutrophication* – 'eu' meaning good or or high, and 'trophic' referring to the nutrient status.

The increased plant growth can have several effects. A growth of algae and larger plants at the water surface can become dense enough to shade out the water below, decreasing plant life in the lower levels of the water. In addition, a prolific growth of plants when decaying and rotting in the autumn can use up oxygen during the decay process as the organic carbon is converted to carbon dioxide. This lack of oxygen can make it difficult for aquatic animals, such as fish, to respire, a condition referred to as *anoxia*. This can be marked in deeper lakes where there is little turnover of the water between the upper oxygenated layers and the deeper layers. It can also occur under ice in winter. As well as increases in plant biomass and subsequent decay, species composition also changes, not only of the algae and of the larger plants but also of the fish species. Larger numbers of smaller fish tend to occur, especially of the smaller herbivorous fish.

As well as nitrate additions, however, other factors can be important, such as the rate of water flow, the depth of the water and the presence of absence of other nutrients. Slow-flowing water tends to increase the problems as there is less circulation of fresh oxygenated water. In terms of other nutrients, if nitrogen is abundant, phosphate tends to become the next important limiting factor and growth is often controlled by phosphate supply in the waters with abundant nitrogen.

Phosphate is strongly adsorbed in the soil and even if added in a fertiliser (as a nitrogen: phosphorous: potassium fertiliser) there is little movement of soluble phosphate into streams. The main mechanism for phosphate movement into streams from agricultural land is the movement of sediment during soil erosion and the desorption of phosphate from the sediment. This is most marked under anaerobic conditions. Oxidised sediments tend to retain phosphate, however. Thus there are two important forms of phosphate: that adsorbed on sediments and unavailable to plants; and the phosphate dissolved in water, termed *soluble reactive phosphate* (SRP), which is immediately available to plants. Thus, while sediment from soil erosion is a source of phosphate, it is only a slowly available source of SRP. The principle sources of SRP are, in fact, often not from soil erosion, but from sewage works and also from dung and slurry from farmyards and stock pens. Sewage is especially high in phosphate, where it is derived from digested plant material, washing liquids and powders and other household sources.

The important point here is that while nitrate may lead to increased plant growth, an increase in plant growth does not necessarily mean that nitrate is the cause of the plant growth. Increased phosphate levels from sewage or agricultural sources may be equally important or more important than nitrate sources. Care thus has to be take before any interpretations about the causes of plant growth are made – eutrophication may be caused by sewage effluent as much as by nitrate.

Nitrate can also have adverse effects on health. If nitrate-rich water is used for drinking purposes, problems may exist in that high nitrate levels in drinking water have been associated with the occurrence of stomach cancer and a condition of babies which can be fatal, termed *methaemoglobinaemia* (blue baby syndrome).

The evidence for these effects is, however, different and somewhat conflicting in the two cases. In the case of stomach cancer, it is known that compounds called nitrosamines are carcinogenic. The possibility exists that nitrates can be converted to nitrosamines in the digestive tract. However, the evidence of any actual effect is conflicting. There are clear cases reported where there are high nitrate levels in drinking water and high levels of stomach cancer. Equally, however, there are areas with high nitrate in drinking water and a low incidence of stomach cancer. Maps can be produced showing the spatial correlation between stomach-cancer incidence and nitrate in drinking water. The flaw in this approach is that nitrate levels refer to the current conditions while cancers may take 30 years to develop and so maps of nitrate levels over the last 30 years might be more appropriate. Thus, there is no clear evidence of a link but since also the possibility exists of a link, it is true to say that there is no proof that no link exists.

In the case of methaemoglobinaemia, the evidence for the effect is clear, though the number of actual cases in the UK is small. The condition is found only in young babies where nitrite is formed in the gut from nitrate and absorbed in the bloodstream, reducing its oxygen-carrying capacity. The baby then appears blue from lack of oxygen. The effect has been shown to occur in rats when nitrate in drinking water reaches high levels, about 100 mg l^{-1} NO_3.

This observation has lead to the safe limit for drinking water being fixed at half this level, 50 mg l^{-1} NO_3. This nitrate concentration can also be expressed as the concentration of nitrate-nitrogen ($NO_3 - N$), that is at 11.3 mg l^{-1} $NO_3 - N$. The actual occurrence of blue babies is rare in Britain because of water treatment to remove nitrate and/or the dispensing of bottled low-nitrate water to babies where there are high nitrate levels in drinking water. A greater problem may exist where there are no mains supplies and local water supplies, such as wells, are not tested regularly by water authorities.

In the matter of human health, the causal links are not clear in the case of stomach cancer, and the significance of the problem, in terms of the lack of widespread effect, is not recognised in the case of blue babies. This has given rise to two reactions. The World Health Organisation (WHO) has introduced regulations concerning water quality, while the agricultural lobby has stressed the uncertainties. In the case of eutrophication and ecological effects, the role of phosphate makes the direct link with agriculture arguable.

Finally, we turn to the problem of lead. Lead is present in leaded petrol and also in some other substances like old paints. One significant source is from lead piping in older houses. It can also be introduced into the environment by smelting plants. It can be found in water supplies and foodstuffs and it can be ingested by children who place dirt in their mouths. Causal uncertainty is minimal but the arguments stem from the derivation of safe levels of lead in the environment and from investment inertia. Thus, a knowledge barrier exists in terms of knowing enough about the levels at which effects become significant and especially in knowing enough about levels of intake and monitoring them. Enaction of policies is thus difficult when sources can be many, monitoring intake is difficult and there are cost implications of improvements.

Leaded petrol is a major source of lead in urban areas, and urban roadside soil can contain up to 3000 $\mu g\ kg^{-1}$. About 95 per cent of the lead in the atmosphere is man-made. Lead is added to petrol to improve the smooth running of engines. Petrol engines have higher power outputs and use fuel more efficiently at high compression but at these compressions smooth running can only be achieved by adding lead compounds. About 75 per cent of the lead added to petrol is dispersed into the atmosphere. This is a particular hazard in housing near areas of high traffic density.

Lead was used for water pipes extensively in the UK until the 1950s. In soft-water areas lead is soluble and concentrations can rise to 1000 $\mu g\ l^{-1}$. The extent of the problem can be assessed by the examination of figures for 1985, when EC standards on drinking water, specifying a maximum lead content of 50 $\mu g\ l^{-1}$, came into force in the UK. It was estimated then that more than 7.5 million people were at risk from lead in drinking water. The cities affected included Birmingham, Liverpool, Manchester, Hull and especially Glasgow.

In areas next to industries which produce lead air-pollution, levels up to 20 000 $\mu g\ kg^{-1}$ can be found in food plants. These levels can give rise to accumulations in the bodies of people regularly eating food plants from the local area. Lead can be present in some paints, and children chewing at paintwork may be at risk. The effects can be particularly marked in young children because of their greater exposure to intake if they ingest soil or paint with a high lead content and because of their greater metabolic rate, resulting in the inhalation of two to three times more pollutants (per unit of body weight) than adults. Lead has also been used as a roofing material and roof drainage water may contain detectable levels of lead which will enter the drain system and ultimately streams and the sea and also, therefore, seafood.

Lead shot also forms a significant environmental hazard when used as a fishing weight. The lead pellets can be ingested by swans together with grit used to grind the food in the gizzard. The extent of the problem can be assessed from the fact that some 3000 swans of an estimated British population of 20 000 die annually (1985 data) from lead poisoning.

What we learn from these examples is, in essence, that unless we can pinpoint the precise nature of the problem, its causes and its effects, we cannot hope to devise a solution. The role of science is to provide such information and if it is lacking, then a considerable knowledge barrier exists. However, we can also see that knowledge barriers can take many forms: was it really CFCs causing the hole in the ozone layer or was it volcanic gases – and if both, in what proportion? How does the mechanism work – how is ozone destroyed by CFCs? How much nitrate leaches from fields? What are the relative contributions of nitrate and phosphate to eutrophication? Are there sources of nitrate other than fertiliser? What is going to be the most effect target to tackle? How much lead do people ingest, and from what sources? Thus, there can be many specific questions. Again, we can attempt to place these questions into a systematic framework of possible barriers so that we can assess whether or not each type of barrier exists when tackling individual problems.

Specifying Knowledge Barriers

Types of Knowledge Barrier

We have already suggested that the first steps in environmental problem-solving include the overcoming of problem denial or, if a problem is recognised, overcoming problem rejection. The denial and rejection stem largely from perspectives, value systems, vested interests and the significance placed on the problem. If these barriers are overcome, and the problem is accepted, then other barriers may be operating, and the first of these to be considered is the knowledge barrier.

The question, then, is whether or not knowledge is adequate for tackling the problem. The barrier is one of being able to identify appropriate management actions which will be effective and thus *we have to understand the causes involved and also the mechanisms and process links between an undesirable effect and its causes*.

There is also the question of *side-effects* to consider, in that we need to know enough about a system so that management actions taken to tackle one problem do not also have damaging subsidiary effects and cause yet further problems. Thus *knowledge barriers involve limitations of our understanding of environmental systems and of our understanding of cause and effect relationships*.

They have three specific contexts, and although all of can be influenced by social and personal attitudes, they represent core tasks for environmental scientists:

1. *Causal identification*: can the causes of the accepted problem be adequately established by the scientific community?
2. *Target definition*: can the instigators of these causes be identified?
3. *Resolution mechanisms*: do we have enough appropriate knowledge to propose effective resolutions within social constraints and without causing side-effects and further problems?

These contexts give rise to three considerations. First, *is there adequate scientific evidence about the causes of the problem to act on?* In particular, there needs to be agreement that the causes have been adequately demonstrated, so that causal uncertainty can be overcome. It should also be borne in mind that the 'evidence' may be viewed differently by different interest groups. Thus we have two facets of *knowledge adequacy* which are involved in overcoming causal uncertainty: *evidence existence* and *evidence interpretation*.

Second, *has the knowledge been gathered in a way that is appropriate to tackling the problem?* The knowledge may have been gained in a variety of ways, not all of them related to environmental goals or ideals, nor necessarily appropriate to the practical needs of environmental managers, nor necessarily in a way that reflects how whole environmental systems work. We can term this *knowledge appropriateness*.

Third, *has the knowledge been adequately communicated to those who intend to tackle the problem?* Knowledge may exist but it may not be communicated adequately to those who need it. This, then, is a question of *knowledge communication*.

We can also suggest not only that did problem denial and problem rejection occur because of the prejudicial attitudes discussed above but also that *problem dismissal* can also occur subsequent to problem acceptance due to such attitudes and due to a perceived lack of adequate evidence.

The Nature of Evidence

Two factors are important here. The first concerns how research is conducted, especially whether it is, or indeed should be, conducted in order to gain evidence and to facilitate management decisions. The second concerns how the available information is interpreted.

Is science dispassionate?

It is important to examine the claim that science is dispassionate – one view of physical/biological scientists is that they carry out their work dispassionately and present the results to society in a clinical or objective package for evaluation and possible action. It can also argued, however, that quite often the type of science which is carried out has a strong influence upon management plans and that the ethos of the scientist is therefore as important as the political will of the practitioner. In addition, there is a view that science merely does what it is told to do by the social and/or economic authority.

We should therefore discuss the view that while the methods of science may be dispassionate, their contexts of operation may not be. The selection of the topic to work on, in a scientific context, may prejudge the type of answer that will be presented to practitioners. There is thus, for example, a questioning by some environmentalists about the morality of research on the burial of nuclear waste at terrestrial sites because any such successful research makes the promotion of nuclear power more feasible. This argument is that nuclear power produces unacceptable wastes and therefore research effort should be directed away from nuclear waste disposal to work on cleaner, alternative sources of energy, such as wind power. Research thus may facilitate a particular line of management. It may also be undertaken to find support for a particular course of action or inaction. Such selectivity in research may result from individual decisions by particular scientists or groups of scientists or to the availability of funding for particular lines of enquiry as constrained by research-funding councils, governments and other research policy-makers. These constraints and pressures will be reacted to in a variety of ways by the spectrum of scientists. Some may strive for what they see as the higher ideals of independent research, others can work within such constraints or they may respond willingly to these pressures and see themselves as addressing important applied issues of the day.

Evidence Interpretation: Prejudice and Causal Uncertainty

Not only is the selection of topics by scientists for research an important factor to consider; the way in which available information is used by particular interest groups is also a fundamental consideration. The key point in this is the significance of evidence. The formulation of evidence is often seen as falling in the domain of science but its use is very much part of the social domain of attitudes and is loaded with value judgements. Many of the bodies which take management decisions and which, for example, might have been accused of causing pollution, may say that they need appropriate scientific evidence before they will act in ameliorating a perceived problem. They thus may well take an '*innocent until proved guilty*' stance, that the burden of proof lies in showing that there is a cause or link involved. Environmental groups often feel that where there is doubt or a probable link, we should act to limit or to prevent possible deleterious effects, and that the burden of proof lies in showing that there is not a causal link. They thus may adopt a '*guilty until proved innocent*' stance.

For example, environmental groups may argue that there is a cancer risk to people living near nuclear power plants and thus the latter are undesirable. Often they can gain evidence to support their case. Management may require more incontrovertible proof of the effect before acting in a way that might impair their interests or involve the spending of public money. The problem may then be that a 'call for action' approach can be dismissed by those implicated in acting on the problem because there is insufficient proof.

But finding incontrovertible proof may be difficult. One reason for this is that scientific research often makes issues more complicated, rather than clarifying them. This is often because the real world is a complex place; in our example of cancers in the vicinity of nuclear power plants, cancers can result from many causes other than radiation, including genetic propensities (Milne, 1989), occupational factors, diet and a variety of environmental factors. It is these other reasons which are often quoted in defence of inaction. There is also the question whether there is a genuine doubt over the cause or a more cynical stance of playing up any uncertainty as a reason for inaction because action will cost a lot of money. The point is that environmental problems often involve multiple factors and therefore any one causal target can duck the issue by playing on the other causes. The problem of evidence is especially difficult where *synergistic* effects are involved. Here, single factors, in themselves, may not be significant but it may be the combined effects of several single causes which add up to a problem. The demand is therefore for science to work in an integrated fashion and to attempt to partition causal effects within an interacting set of factors. With a more dissective approach of specifying individual causes, it may not be possible to achieve an overall picture both of multiple causes and of how they interact. This *causal partitioning* represents a substantial challenge to science and a major knowledge barrier.

As an example, it may be known that agriculturally applied pesticides could kill fish in lakes within an agricultural catchment, but if fish disappear in a lake this does not necessarily mean that pesticides are to blame. An effect can be produced by many different causes and the fish might have been affected by a parasite or by toxic waste from an industrial plant, or by overfishing, or by cold winters or by some complex interaction of several factors. Again, the agriculturalist would need strong evidence of blame before taking alternative actions, especially if these were more costly. Again, environmentalists might argue the case for preventative action because there was an evident risk. Only if there were a common interest, such as would be the case if pesticide losses were costly to the farmer and also known to cause harm to fish which the farmer also profited from, would the need for strong evidence be less.

Acid rain is another example and one which we have cited before. While it is thought that sulphur dioxide (SO_2) from industrial smokestacks can increase rainfall acidity and this, in turn, can have a detrimental effect on tree growth, decreased tree growth in itself is no proof of the direct effects of acid rain, since it can be due to a number of causes, including insect infestation or complex chemical reactions in the atmosphere involving nitrogen oxides (NO_x) from car exhausts and atmospheric ozone. Investment in technology to reduce sulphur dioxide emissions from industry may not, then, improve forest growth if the real cause is car exhaust fumes; again, strong evidence would be needed before money was spent on fitting desulphurising scrubbers to smokestacks. However, strong evidence for the effects of individual sources may not be forthcoming if the environmental effects have multiple, interacting causes.

Evidence about causes and sources is distinct from arguments over evidence of effects, which we discussed in Chapter 3. For example, Friends of the Earth, argued with the Forestry Commission in the mid-1980s over the extent of forest damage in the UK, each quoting different figures for the proportion of trees damaged. This is situation uncertainty; but once agreement between the two sides was reached, and the existence of forest damage was accepted, (see: Cape *et al.*, 1988) the issue became, as above, one of causal uncertainty – was it acid rain and if so was it due to sulphur dioxide, car exhausts or ozones, or some combination of these and/or some other factor?

Thus, there can be major problems with gaining evidence about causes. Causality can be complex and science is not necessarily used dispassionately. It can be used to support the case for inaction, saying that other causes are involved if there is any doubt about cause and effect. If science seeks the truth, the truth is often more complicated than any protagonist would like it to be. Thus, gaining evidence can provide a significant barrier because the complexities of natural situations often make it difficult to identify clearly the causal factors involved. These complexities can form a significant barrier to agreeing on the nature and causes of a problem and to providing a clear knowledge base for action.

Adequate Knowledge

Adequate knowledge for management thus covers several aspects, so we have to ask what constitutes adequate knowledge. It clearly includes not only a general knowledge of processes, but also a knowledge of how the processes are combined at specific sites to produce particular effects and consequent clear identification of the target causes.

It also covers the topic of what the likely consequences of actions are going to be. It may be thought, before an action is taken, that our knowledge is adequate and that we have identified the causal factors. But if this knowledge is based on predictive modelling or laboratory testing, it can fall short of the way in which systems behave in nature under the test of actual implementation. Quite often, the misfiring of plans under management is the only evidence we have that our knowledge was, in fact, inadequate, and the situation is not improved because we have misidentified the target cause. Additionally, there may be some unforeseen side-effects. Thus, actions may have been taken in good faith, but the results were unexpected and an action taken to solve one problem may not only fail to solve it but also give rise to others. Scientific research therefore needs to evaluate the implications of various alternative management actions not only for the target cause but also in spheres other than the management target, both before and during management implementation.

The Ways in Which Scientists Work

The Type of Knowledge and Scientific Approaches

The kinds of knowledge we have available for environmental management depend very much on how we go about gaining it, in terms of both general philosophy and specific techniques and methods. Three main areas of tension between the gaining of scientific knowledge and the needs of environmental management are involved. First, there is the tension between, on the one hand, the philosophy that management actions should be seen in the context of the environment as a whole – and thus that they need a basis of information of a *holistic*, interactive nature – and, on the other, the fact that much of science is *dissective* and compartmentalised in nature.

Second, the kind of information relevant to tackling a problem at a particular site, and especially assessments of particular combinations of causative factors, are often site-specific, whereas science can often be seen as producing general laws and fundamental principles which are not site-specific.

Third, some scientific methodologists assert that falsification (refutation of hypotheses by experiment and observation) is the only defensible form of proceeding – as opposed to verification (amassing observations that tend to confirm a hypothesis). Quite apart from the fact that many scientists, in fact, adopt a verification procedure rather than a falsification one, environmental management needs not only a knowledge of what is not important and what will not work, but also a body of positive, verified evidence about linkages and causes on which to base management actions.

A Holistic Approach

The investigation of the environment as a whole system is crucial to the tackling of environmental problems because many transcend the boundaries of specialist investigation and because management actions have far wider ramifications than the intended target: the environment responds as a whole when stressed at a particular point. Thus a holistic approach is necessary to understand how the environment interreacts as a whole.

Traditionally, we see environmental systems as complex phenomena, with many factors operating in complicated, multi-faceted interrelationships. Our common reaction to this is to be dissective, and to break down environmental processes into small compartments. If a scientist is to tackle a problem of manageable size, the research topic often has to be defined and limited in some way, either by specialising in subject matter and limiting the breadth of factors considered or by taking a more general approach involving interrelationships, but often at the expense of detail. The former, traditional, dissective, specialist approach to environmental components does not provide us with information about how whole systems might react under management actions. It also promotes a partial, limited approach to management actions whereby an action is taken to tackle one particular situation without due regard for the wider ramifications of that action. With a broader approach, loss of specialist detail may occur and, moreover, experimental evidence is difficult to gain. A holistic approach to whole systems, with both breadth and specialist detail, while it may be more desirable, becomes very unwieldy. Thus we are often only able to use systems models to characterise whole systems in terms of major inputs, outputs and processes and to act as a basis for management.

Clearly, what is needed is rigourous scientific research on whole systems, involving large-scale control experimentations. Such an approach acts to reduce the tensions between scientific research and management because false ideas can be eliminated by experiment and observation and the consequences of actions can be demonstrated and modelled by approaching whole systems in a scientific manner and in a way that is useful to managers.

Notwithstanding the importance of whole-system experimentation, however, it is often seen as difficult to use factorial experimental design in the investigation of whole systems, if not impossible. The factorial experiment

– where only the factors of interest are varied and all other factors are kept as constant as possible – is a very reasonable way to proceed. This approach can provide fundamental theories about relationships which may be applied to a wide variety of situations. However, in large systems, replication and control are often impossible and, in nature, many factors operate together in a way that is different from how they operate in isolation under control conditions.

We are often only left with the option of computer modelling of whole systems in order to study the likely consequences of management actions. Computer simulation of climatic changes and projections of the relationships between population and resources (see Meadows, 1972) are good examples of this approach. However, we are only then dealing with probabilities and any model predictions are only as good as the information and assumptions fed into the models. In addition, no management action effects can be 100 per cent predicted because, quite apart from assessments of predictive success depending on what are the criteria for measuring success, we are always operating in a state of partial knowledge. There is also the point that the longer a system operates, the more complex and difficult to predict it becomes. For example, a weather forecast can be accurate for the next six hours, but is less so for the next six days. Such limitations, then, can provide major barriers to solving environmental problems involving major-scale issues – of both a spatial and temporal nature.

One of the few situations where we do get near to a 'whole-system' experiment is large-scale water-catchment experiments which involve contrasting treatments of replicate areas (Trudgill, 1988). Here, entire replicate catchments or watersheds are instrumented on similar rock types and soils and under similar climatic conditions, but land use is varied, with, for example, plantations of coniferous trees or the retention of deciduous forests. Then different management strategies are applied, such as a comparison of wholesale and selective felling strategies, a variety of road-building strategies and a variety of herbicide-application strategies, to determine the effects of different management treatments on water yield and on sediment and solute outputs. These large-scale experiments involve effective control of management variables in realistic situations. They can, therefore, give the most useful results on how whole systems behave under management. However, they are costly and labour-intensive to set up. They are also limited to the catchment scale and cannot consider cross-catchment transfers and interactions or broader-scale effects such as climate.

If the resources of time, money and land are not available for such large-scale experimentation, the approach remains one of smaller-scale, specialist research and the building-up of ideas about whole-system processes, coupled with a broader systems modelling for large-scale effects where experimental design is inappropriate. Often it is this body of accumulated wisdom that practitioners use when drawing up management plans. Thus management tends to be based on a 'rule of thumb' approach to how things are thought to work, rather than on the results of experimental tests.

We can conclude that a major knowledge barrier is where the kind of knowledge we have is inadequate because it is not broad enough in scope. If we have knowledge in depth, it may well be limited in breadth of application. Often we lack knowledge of interactions at a large scale must fall back on a modelling approach, which is a lot better than nothing but is only as good as the assumptions we feed in. Clearly, apart from some large-scale catchment testing, often the only tests we have of such models is by operationalising them – which may or may not tackle a problem, although it will almost certainly improve our understanding of interrelationships.

Generalisation and Site-Specific Research

It is often agreed that the purpose of science is to generalise laws and theories. But working on fundamental processes to gain knowledge which could be applied in a number of contexts differs from working on the identification of causes in specific instances. The former, fundamental, work is often seen as more important by science because it endeavours to evaluate universal principles. However, while essential for basic understanding, this is not all that environmental management needs.

This is because a problem can have a specific location and combination of factors which have to be evaluated for that site or issue and thus applied work is often essential to address the situation obtaining in a particular problem – and its results may not be applicable elsewhere. So if a piece of research is undertaken to unravel a particular problem at a specific location in order to specify the relative importance of various causative factors, the scientific establishment is liable to ask how the results can be transferred to other sites, or whether the results are just locally applicable. However, environmental problems can be very site-specific, with particular combinations of factors and effects.

Thus, there can be tensions between scientific approaches and the needs of environmental managers as environmental management needs to know what happens at particular sites in order to be able to tackle specific problems, as well as referring to general theory. The answer often given to this situation is that general theories or models are under test at that site and that the research is a contribution to general theory, especially by the evaluation of new models or the calibration of existing ones.

But while the calibration of existing models is a useful approach in environmental problem-solving, the relative importance of various contributory factors still has to be evaluated in a site-specific way. We can thus see a barrier which may exist in the sense that the formulation of general theories, while fundamental (and often supported by research-funding bodies), does not necessarily tell us how to tackle a particular problem at a specific site, such are the complexities of interrelationships, which may vary considerably from site to site.

Fundamental work is therefore essential, but site-specific applied work may not have the kudos it deserves in science because it can be addressing particular situations rather than universal principles. This is not to say that applied work, such as environmental problem-solving, is the only justification for the existence of knowledge. Pure inquiry and the satisfying of curiosity are always legitimate goals. In addition, applied work is based on fundamental knowledge, even if this knowledge may have been seemingly unapplied when first acquired. It is also true that the understanding of fundamental process is basic to management since it is more effective, and often cheaper in the long run, to work with nature rather than against it.

Scientists must therefore continue to work on fundamental processes, whether there is an application in view or not, and this should not be lost sight of in attempts to be relevant to society. However, there is pressing societal concern about environmental issues which does mean that they are a legitimate area of endeavour. Thus, neither fundamental work nor site-specific applied work should be neglected because fundamental work is legitimate in itself and provides the basis for applied work and the applied work is necessary to meet the demands and needs of society. What is clear is that a knowledge barrier may exist in terms of a lack of appropriate knowledge if only fundamental principles are known and they are not evaluated and applied to specific problems – especially if such applied, site-specific work is discouraged by the scientific establishment.

Scientific Method

Not only can it be suggested that there is a difference between science which seeks to derive fundamental theory and science which seeks to tackle problems at particular places (albeit relying heavily on fundamental theory); there can also be further differences in approaches which scientists say they adopt, approaches which they actually adopt and the approaches which environmental management needs.

Many people who write on the subject of scientific method propose that a *deductive* method of scientific enquiry is the only defensible forms of research. Such method includes the testing of ideas by observation and experiment. This is to say that there is a proposition about how the real world works, derived from previous work and/or intuition, which is then tested using a crucial experimental design in order to see whether or not the proposition can be *falsified*. If it cannot, then it is left open for further testing. Many scientists would pay lip-service to this approach. However, if 'good science' can be seen as the falsification of ideas about how the environment works by rigorous experimental design, this is not necessarily what all scientists do, nor is it always what practical managers need.

Many research workers, rather than adopting a *falsification* procedure, proceed via *verification*, whereby evidence builds up to fit a theory, the conclusions often being that 'it appears to work like this . . . ', rather than 'we have refuted this and this possibility, leaving others open for testing'. Many also undertake descriptive non-experimental observations which are not nested in a problem-solving context. Nor does discovery always come from the strict application of directed hypothesis testing; it often comes incidentally while working on something else. Scientific methodology purists would tend to reject this point of view, although they might recognise that many people work in this way.

A verification approach is often regarded as philosophically indefensible since no matter how many cases fit in with a proposed theory, there always remains the possibility of a case, as yet unfound, which will refute the theory. Despite this, there are innumerable papers in the scientific literature which have not involved falsification, perhaps because it is seen as irrelevant, too impractical or because the philosophical standpoint is simply ignored. Instead, research workers accumulate knowledge about how a system appears to work. This can be especially true of approaches to large systems, where the control of variables in replicated situations is often difficult to effect.

The relationship between science and management is an important one because often, in reality, practitioners are essentially drawing upon hypotheses which have not yet been refuted. A lack of experimental evidence or implementation testing can clearly be a source of management problems because there will always be the possibility that managers have got it wrong. The managers feel that there is sufficient evidence, in a verification sense, on which to base their actions, and this is supported by evident scientific approaches, but these are often merely accumulated cases which fit in with particular theories. If, in fact, the actions are really based on as yet unrefuted hypotheses, then it can indeed be seen that there is great scope for mismanagement. Even if there is past experience of actions which have worked successfully in other places, they may not work in another. Verification is weak, as there always remains the possibility of a case, as yet unfound, which will refute the theory. It can readily be seen that management actions on large systems are in many ways often the only tests of hypotheses about how such systems work, only providing evidence on whether or not our ideas are right once they are put into action. This is a pragamatic approach of accumulated evidence and trial and error. The novelist John Steinbeck (1960) observed this when he wrote: 'Science never proves anything, it makes guesses and goes by them as long as they work well.'

If it is accepted that a defensible scientific method involves falsification, it is possible to observe that this approach is not necessarily helpful if strictly applied if it only tells us what does not work, rather than providing guidelines for management; hence there can be a tension between scientific method and management. 'Good science' (falsification) is necessary to eliminate erroneous ideas, certainly, but this merely leaves options open on other ideas. So, on the one hand, some scientists are saying that falsification is the only defensible approach to science, while, on the other, such an approach does not necessarily produce positive guidelines for management – these tend to be based on verification and the accumulation of evidence. The problem with this is that there can always be a case where the ideas do not work, the management action having provided only a further test of the ideas, and this, if we have got it wrong, can have deleterious consequences for the environment.

It can be argued, then, that there are problems with a rational approach to management based on the rigorous application of scientific method as proposed by some advocates. In addition, management is not always placed wholly, if at all, in a rational context – political considerations often have a greater influence on management decisions than scientific knowledge, let alone the outcome of strict hypothesis testing. There is perhaps more tension, then, between scientific methodology purists and scientists than there is between the scientists involved in verification, and managers, such as engineers. Frequently, simple descriptions of states are the only 'scientific' steps involved, together with value judgements on the desirability of the states. Here, the arguments become more ones of perception, aesthetics and social pressures. This is not to say that scientific work on processes should not be important, but that frequently, in the real world, it may be ignored or take second place to more emotional arguments. If science is involved in any way, then it may be solely in terms of a descriptive *survey* of, say, the number of flowers or birds which might be adversely affected by a proposed management. Thus, management plans may be implemented or quashed irrespective of scientific knowledge about processes and system linkages, though such a knowledge is usually seen by scientists as a fundamental basis for rational management.

It can be argued that managers need a body of accumulated, positive evidence which can be used as a basis in formulating their policies, which are then implemented within a societal value system, rather than a series of tests which have falsified various options. Falsification is a crucial step in the negative sense of eliminating those courses of actions which are irrelevant or which will definitely have deleterious effects, but more is required – positive statements of what should be done, what will work and what the outcomes of various alternative actions could be at particular sites, or in the context of a particular problem, and within a holistic, mutually reactive ecosystem.

The fact that science can be dissective, strive for fundamental principles, and not be site- or problem-specific enables us to understand our knowledge barriers in more depth.

It is also clear that as well as the perceived needs of being dissective and addressing universality, science should be holistic; as well as providing general principles or laws it should provide site- or problem-specific knowledge and effective guidelines for management – the latter point concerns the need for developing wisdom rather than just providing knowledge.

The Communication of Knowledge

In some cases, adequate knowledge may exist but it is not communicated to those who need it. Much scientific knowledge is present in scientific journals and books but if practitioners do not have access to this knowledge, then this can lead to the lack of implementation of solutions.

This is especially true where the practitioners are a large number of dispersed individuals who do not necessarily have good communications with each other or with the scientific establishment, like farmers (especially in the less-developed countries), rather than when they are a coherent body or institution. It is also a matter of targeting the appropriate outlets. Thus, for example, there are hundreds of useful research papers in scientific establishments concerning agriculture and environment, but unless the information appears suitably expressed in outlets such as the *Farmer's Weekly* or is transmitted to the individual farmer through agricultural advisers, then this is tantamount to the information not existing. In the context of tropical agriculture, Pereira (1981) was able to conclude, when writing about tropical agricultural hydrology: 'In both Asia and Africa I have heard frequently statements that "there is no data on the effects of X and Y" when the lack could be remedied by a week or two in a good library.' Notwithstanding a touch of arrogance in this statement (few tropical farmers have access to 'good libraries'!), it is clear that there is a communication barrier to the dissemination of knowledge which does exist. This barrier is related to the willingness and ability of scientists to transmit their information in a suitable fashion as much as it is to the education and literacy of those who might use it.

As a further example, it has been known for several years that certain pesticides applied agriculturally can have deleterious environmental and human effects. Yet Bull (1982) has been able to document their continued use in many parts of the Third World. Here, it is not the lack of knowledge which gives rise to the problems, it is more a matter of the dominance of social, economic and political factors, inadequate legislation and lack of communication of the knowledge which lead to their continued use.

Often at research conferences, the claim that 'further work is necessary' can be heard coming from physical, chemical and biological scientists. This is often true, especially in specifying the cause and effect links in particular combinations of circumstances and factors at specific locations, but increasingly, if effective implementation of environmental solutions is to occur, then the further work should involve communication networks within social, economic and political frameworks.

Another aspect of this may be that adequate knowledge exists and every other aspect is right for solution implementation, but that it may take time for the solution to be implemented – again communication and education are important factors here (as discussed in Chapter 6).

Knowledge Barriers: A Summary

We can summarise this chapter by suggesting that knowledge barriers can be of three main types. First, there are the more practical ones where knowledge, in the form of evidence about causes, may or may not exist (casual uncertainty) and where, even if it is does, there may be varied interpretations of its adequacy. Problem dismissal can thus stem, quite legitimately, from causal uncertainty, or it can stem from prejudices, vested interests, perspectives or value systems despite causal clarification, and indeed the latter prejudicial system can play on the former uncertainty. In other words, adequate knowledge *may not* exist, forming a barrier of genuine or, cynically, convenient doubt (a *knowledge-existence* barrier), or it *may* exist, but be ignored (*a knowledge-interpretation or -significance* barrier).

Second, there are the more philosophical points that science may not gain the types of knowledge most appropriate to causal clarification or for resolution proposal. This may be because the knowledge is not holistic enough or because, while perfectly valid in scientific terms, it is gained in such a way as not to provide clear enough guidelines for practical management. These are *knowledge appropriateness* barriers.

Third, there may exist a perfectly appropriate and useful body of knowledge, but it may not be communicated to those who need it to make a rational decision. This is *a knowledge communication* barrier.

These can be overcome by research to minimise causal uncertainty; demonstrating the significance of the causal evidence to those involved to minimise problem dismissal; ensuring that research is appropriate to the problems, especially by establishing the legitimacy of problem-solving research, which is often site-specific, in the scientific community; and by improving the communication of appropriate knowledge. If such barriers are overcome, we may now, perhaps, agree on the problem (problem acceptance) and can identify the causes sufficiently to propose management action (resolution proposal).

These points can be summarised in diagrammatic form (Figure 4.2). From problem acceptance we move to the existence of *evidence of causes*, gained according to the value systems of scientists. This may then be interpreted as not only positive or negative relative to a case that may be made but also as *adequate* or *inadequate*. Causal uncertainty, often due to the complexities of situations, can lead to problem dismissal. The only solution to this is further research, which may increase the realisation of complexity or lead to clarification. If the causes can be clarified, or if evidence is already seen as adequate, *targets* can be *defined* and *resolutions proposed*.

The next steps involve those which intervene between *resolution proposal* and *resolution implementation* and may involve economic, social and political factors. We shall return to consider these steps more in Chapter 6, but the first question is whether we have the means to implement a solution. Technological barriers are the subject of the next chapter.

Figure 4.2 Summary of the stages leading to resolution proposal. Knowledge barriers which have to be overcome are the provision of evidence, clarification of causes and definition of targets for action. Problem dismissal (shaded) can relate to causal uncertainty and vested interests; both have to be overcome before a resolution can be proposed.

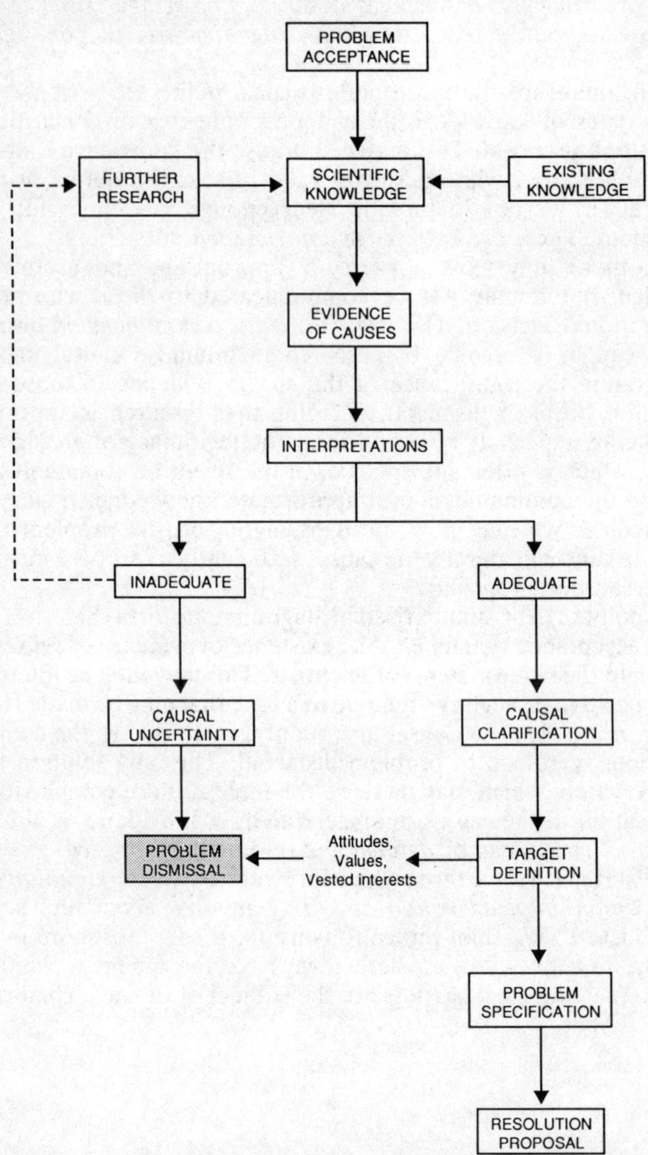

Chapter 5
Technological Barriers

Do We Have Technological Solutions to All Our Problems?

If we have recognised and accepted a problem, the issue then becomes one of whether we have the means to tackle it. As with knowledge barriers, the questions of technological barriers concern existence and appropriateness.

Lack of some kind of technology rarely proves to be a barrier, however, once problem acceptance has been reached. We seem to be very good at devising methods for solving problems once they have been accepted, and it is also probably true to say that there are many more methods available for tackling problems than there are in actual use. Referring back to our ozone-depletion, nitrate and lead examples, there exist propellants other than CFCs; there exist slow-release fertilisers and methods of extracting nitrate from water; and there are alternatives to lead pipes (copper, plastic) and to lead in petrol. It is the implementation and the economic, social and political implications of alternative technologies which often provide the stumbling blocks.

This is a fundamental point about environmental problem-solving – it often happens either that we are stuck in disagreement over whether a problem is a problem, and whether it matters, or that we know what the problem is and we know what do to but we do nothing because of economic, social or political factors. Technological limitations rarely provide a barrier because once a need has been recognised, somebody, somewhere, will come up with a means of meeting that need, especially if there is some financial gain to be made in so doing. Thus, often a technology exists somewhere for solving a problem if only we could agree that it needed tackling and we could implement it in a social context; and if a technology does not already exist, it soon will.

In many cases, however, the appropriateness of the technology can be questioned. The questions involved are whether the technology is appropriate for the society involved, in that it should not impair the social fabric of that society; whether the means is self-sustaining and not exploitative of scarce resources; and whether the way is capital-intensive, creating financial dependency and indebtedness. These are much more crucial issues than whether a means exists or not, especially as many inappropriate technological 'solutions' are often seen as a cause of environmental problems rather than a cure for them.

Thus technological barriers concern not so much finding any means as finding the right means, and being able to evaluate what 'right' is.

The suggestion that we often have technological answers to problems (and we shall examine this for specific issues below) does, however, need qualification. There is a point of view which claims that we need not worry about environmental problems because we will always be able to find technological solutions to them. This has been termed the *technological fix* approach to problems.

This should be treated with caution because it denies the existence of prejudices, vested interests and value systems which, as we have seen, can lead to problem denial, rejection and dismissal (see Figures 3.2, 3.3 and 4.2) – and this is despite the existence of many technological means of solution. It misses the point that technical means may be necessary but they are not sufficient for problem solution and that there are many other factors which prevent us from solving environmental problems. It can give rise to a form of complacency that somehow we can go on exploiting and destroying the life-support base, that when the crunch comes we will be able to 'fix' it, but that until that state is reached we need not worry.

It also implies the arrogant point of view that we know best about the environment and how natural systems work and thus that when natural systems break down, we can replace them with systems of our own which will work just as well or better. This misses the point that it is easier and cheaper to work with nature in the long run and that there will be a cost involved in our own 'technological fixes'. For example, if water supplies are polluted, we can counter this by all having water purifiers; if water supplies are polluted with nitrate, we can fix this by having denitrification plants (estimated in 1987 to cost around £15 billion for the UK alone). It would, in fact, be better not to fix the damage caused by pollution but to tackle it at source and prevent it from occurring, as discussed in Chapter 3.

Similarly, it is suggested that the destruction of the tropical rainforest is assisting the increase of carbon dioxide levels in the atmosphere. This is because trees assimilate carbon dioxide during photosynthesis and a dwindling forest cover means less assimilation. This, it is said, will lead to an atmospheric warming because of the way in which carbon dioxide reflects radiation back to the earth's surface. While accepting this problem, a suggested 'fix' is to plant hundreds of square miles of fast-growing trees in order to absorb the extra carbon dioxide. This is a neat solution and has mathematical appeal. But we are being carried away by our own cleverness; this approach misses the points about the sanctity of the rainforest, its ecological riches and our roles of stewardship and responsibility for irreplaceable ecosystems on the earth. As Oliver Rackham (1986) has it, removing old hedgerows and replanting new ones is akin to 'burning a picture by Constable and substituting it with a good forgery'.

So we have two conclusions so far: we can fix many problems by using already available and new techniques, but we have to think whether this is desirable. We ought to adopt a more humble approach of working with nature rather than destroying it and then being clever enough to replace it with something of our own, both at a financial cost to ourselves and at a cost to the environment. The other conclusion is that it is possible that the very existence of technological solutions – and our confidence in them – actually promotes rather solves environmental problems. If we feel that we can always fix something, we will not worry about it. This really comes back to the point about the appropriateness of technological solutions rather than whether they exist or not.

Specific Issues

We can now ask whether we have the technologies to solve specific problems, whether these technologies are appropriate, and whether their lack forms a barrier to solution or whether their presence gives rise to complacency over finding a solution. Table 3.1 listed some of the specific issues with which we might be concerned. For most of these issues, technological barriers do not exist, as shown below:

Ozone depletion. Alternative technologies are available to sprays: hand-pressure sprays or alternative propellants.

Overfishing. Nets of larger meshes can be used to prevent the catching of smaller fish before they reach maturity.

Soil erosion. Techniques of conservation include terracing, contouring, minimal cultivation, use of mulching and land survey to identify slopes at risk.

Acid rain. Sulphur dioxide can be elimated at source by scrubbers in chimneys; nitrous oxides can similarly be removed from car exhaust by engine modifications.

Lead pollution. It is possible to remove lead from petrol, paint and industrial emissions.

Radiation. Some technological uncertainty after the Chernobyl incident and radiation leaks from nuclear power plants.

Pesticides. It is possible to farm without them, though at a lower productivity. It is also possible to use those with more specific targets, with shorter decay periods, with less damage to wildlife and people. A limitation lies in keeping pace with pesticide-resistant strains of pest.

Nitrates. There are techniques for minimising agricultural losses by using slow-release (but more expensive) fertilisers, other fertilisers (such as organic matter) and by judicious placement timings. We are able to remove nitrates from water by denitrification.

Eutrophication. Phosphates can be removed from sewage by stripping; phosphate losses from agricultural land can be minimised by controlling soil erosion (phosphate is highly adsorbed on to soil particles) and drainage from stock yards.

Water quality and sewage. We are technologically able to control effluent by the removal of undesirable substances from effluent.

Overpopulation. A number of effective birth-control techniques are available.

Destruction of the countryside, conifer plantation, habitat change, drainage, and urbanisation. Technological limitations are largely irrelevant in the decisions about land-use change but we usually have technological means by which their impacts can be minimised (especially in methods of hedge management, planting and drainage).

We can conclude that the technology is often available for problem solution, though there could be argument about some of the finer points and some of the instances, especially over the containment of nuclear radiation. So it is clear that, in general, technological limitations do not provide barriers to environmental problem-solving, either because of prior existence of the means or by their invention to fill an accepted need.

Appropriateness, complacency, cost and other barriers

If the technologies largely exist, why do we not use them? Simply, it is often a question of cost. This is one reason why complacency about the existence of technical fixes is misguided. The other reasons are, of course, problem denial, rejection and dismissal, based on prejudices or lack of conviction about the evidence, as already discussed, as well as social or political factors.

Environmental Appropriateness

But what of appropriateness? We can see that appropriateness already has a cost factor as a criterion, which also feeds into a general social and political acceptability. Appropriateness for other aspects of the environment is also important. For example, one reason why sulphur scrubbers have not been widely installed in chimneys to reduce acid rain is that they involve the use of calcium carbonate derived from limestone, which would involve more quarrying and landscape destruction. Is sulphur scrubbing an environmentally appropriate technology, then, or would alternatives energy sources be more acceptable? It is true that alternative sources – nuclear, wind, tidal or solar power – also have their environmental implications to a greater or lesser extent and it is then a matter of evaluating which is the least environmentally detrimental and therefore which is the most appropriate.

Nitrate is another issue where appropriateness of the technological solution is an issue. Denitrification of drinking water is possible but this misses the point about the detrimental effects on the ecological state of streams and waterways between farmland and the water-treatment plant. Here eutrophication can substantially alter algal and higher plant growth, causing blooms of algae and choked waterways. When the biomass decays it uses up oxygen, leading to fish suffocation and the impoverishment of aquatic life. It would be better to devise technologies and methods to tackle the nitrate losses at source, either by reduced application of fertiliser or by the use of slower-release fertiliser pellets – which in fact exist, but their cost is currently prohibitive for routine use. As for phosphates, removal from sewage is possible, but at a cost to the water authority – so would it not be more appropriate to use phosphate-free detergent and thus reduce phosphate levels at source?

We can therefore suggest that technology is most appropriate if it tackles the source of the problem, rather than the effects and also if, in itself, it does not lead to further environmental damage.

Social Appropriateness

Further aspects of appropriateness concern social relevance and acceptance. There are many examples, especially in the Third World, where technology has been applied but has only made matters worse. These include costly structures, like dams and boreholes, which increase indebtedness, focus overgrazing in a manner likely to cause vegetation loss and soil erosion, and are difficult to maintain and have the effect of changing the society which they are purporting to help. Simple technologies, easy to maintain, are liable to be more effective and absorbed into the social fabric, rather than altering it.

Positive steps which have improved environmental conditions in Africa through socially appropriate technology are described by the International Institute for Environment and Development (IIED, 1987) and by Paul Harrison (1987). In these books it is shown how conventional development efforts by donors and governments have failed to halt the vicious downward spiral of environmental degradation and deepening poverty, and indeed in some cases have aggravated it. However, a growing number of projects and programmes have succeeded and these can be used to illustrate the nature of socially appropriate technology. Here the problems of pests, fertilisers, food supply, soil erosion and fuel wood have been tackled by appropriate technologies. We can study examples from these writings in order to suggest what the lessons are.

One example concerns the selection of appropriate crop strains. There has been much fruitful work on new strains of sweet potato, maize and sorghum, and the work on cassava in Nigeria has been especially successful. The International Institute of Tropical Agriculture at Ibadan has selected varieties that will succeed under conditions where no fertilisers, pesticides or fungicides have been applied and then tested them in areas with serious soil or disease problems. They have thus developed strains which are resistant to viruses and other major diseases such as blight. This is a key development because these strains require no purchased inputs; and because they are less susceptible to disease, yields are high (300% more than traditional varieties) and sustained from year to year. They are also bushier plants and thus shade the ground more, reducing time spent in weeding. The use of the new strain has spread rapidly, covering an estimated 200,000 hectares by 1983. This development is thus appropriate for the society in that it is independent of expensive outside inputs.

With regard to fertiliser usage, there is a clear indication that the future lies in the use of organic residues rather than with chemical fertilisers. Application of nitrogenous fertilisers is expensive, thus engendering a high financial risk if there is a crop failure. There may also encourage soil acidification and thus also potassium deficiency and aluminium toxicity. Moderate use of phosphate fertiliser is supported as phosphate is deficient in most African soils and can have dramatic results: 15 kilograms triple superphosphate can per hectare double millet yields. However, this is again expensive and the long-term future involves lower-cost measures. These include the use of manures, crop residues and leguminous plants. These involve a low financial input and therefore a low financial risk. They

Figure 5.1 Simple, effective and appropriate technology: stone lines and terraces to control soil erosion (adapted from Pacey and Cullis, 1984).

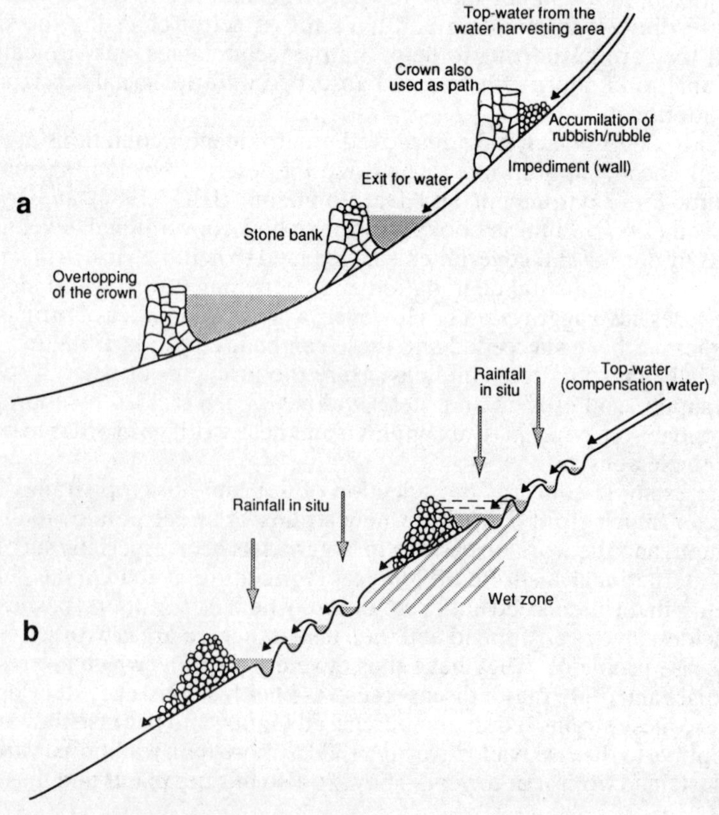

Figure 5.2 Appropriate technology: method of contouring using water filled tubes in order to lay out level stone lines. (a) Wooden stakes with tubes attached are held together and water levels are marked on the stakes (R). (b) Stale A is fixed and B is positioned on the ground some way away till the water level rests a R, A is then at the same level as B. (Adapted from Pacey and Cullis, 1984).

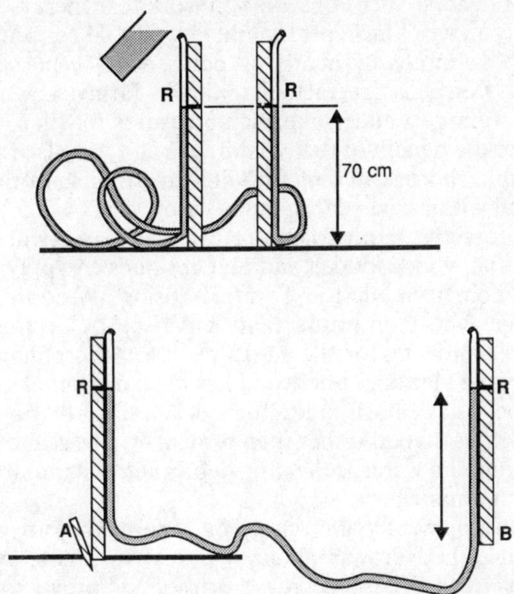

also simultaneously increase production and increase soil conservation – the organic residues improve soil stability by improving soil water infiltration and soil moisture levels. Crop residues can improve yields by 50–60 per cent in humid areas and by as much as 80 per cent in semi-arid areas. This shows that not only that it is possible to have productive agriculture simultaneously with conserving and improving the soil resource, but also that the improvements in the soil actually increase the crop productivity.

Similarly, other schemes in Africa also involve simultaneous conservation and production methods, in particular the use of contour stone lines, terracing and intregrated agroforestry systems. In an Oxfam scheme in Burkina Faso, stone lines (Figure 5.1) are made during the dry season when labour is available and are laid out along the contour. The contours are defined out using a simple U-tube made from transparent tubing (Figure 5.2). Water levels in the tube are used to indicate where the contour lines run and thus the survey method is inexpensive, easily understood and easily applied. The stone lines dam up water running down the slope, decreasing its erosive power and giving the water time to infiltrate. Soil, organic matter and seeds start to collect on the upslope side of the lines and plants begin to grow. The lines take up only 1–2 per cent of the crop land but can increase yields by up 50 per cent.

In Kenya successful terracing programmes involve the use of simple *fanya juu* or 'work up' terraces. Here, a narrow trench is dug out and the soil thrown uphill to form a ridge. Alternative crop residues or a trash of twigs are laid out on the contour. In both cases, slope wash brings soil particles downhill which then collect against the ridge or trash, eventually forming a series of level terraces. Such conservation works can increase crop yields by 30–65 per cent, improve farm profitability by 60–100 per cent, and increase returns on labour inputs by nearly 40 per cent. One particular aspect of the success in Kenya is the fact of tenure – farmers own the land and are therefore willing to undertake such measures for their own long-term benefit, and for the benefit of their children, but it was also found that there was considerable short-term benefit, with investments of time and labour being recouped within one year in many cases.

Integrating forestry with agriculture can also pay dividends, supplying much needed fuelwood, fodder and leaf residues to apply to the land as well as protection from wind and water erosion. Windbreaks have been planted in Niger and crop productivity has risen by up to around 20 per cent, even after allowing for the 12–15 per cent of cropland taken out of production by tree planting. Fuelwood has been marketed successfully and also living fences have been made for stock, rather than wooden fences, which consume dead wood rather than provide it. Trees and shrubs also act as barriers to running water, collecting debris and soil into terraces without any further extra input.

A further development is alley cropping, where crops are grown between regularly pruned hedgerows, about 4–8 metres apart, of fast-growing nitrogen-fixing trees. These decrease erosion, improve soil fertility and regular pruning reduces competition with the crop and provides fodder and organic residues to dig into the soil. Pruning is labour-intensive but saves labour in that time would otherwise have to spend gathering fuelwood and fodder. One particular nitrogen-fixing tree, *Leucaena,* produces up to 6 tonnes of stakes per hectare per year, with 15–20 tonnes of leaves and twigs containing over 160 kilograms of nitrogen, 150 kilograms of potassium and 15 kilograms of phosphorous. These can be applied to the fields and farmers have recorded yield increases of around 40 per cent.

Technical innovations and improvements can also be important, as is illustrated by the use of improved charcoal stoves in Kenya. These offered fuel savings of around 35 per cent, reducing pressures on scarce wood resources. They are constructed from scrap and have an insulating ceramic liner, a built-in grate and ash pan. They last longer than older types and pay for themselves in savings on charcoal purchase within a year – often within a few weeks. Even simpler stove designs can also be used, made from three stones and a clay shield. These also conserve fuel, cost nothing and give a quick return on the small amount of labour invested.

The lessons are clear. Improvements can be and have been made; environmental problems can be tackled successfully. But success is most likely when this is done with the involvement of local people. To be successful, successful schemes must be small-scale and fit in with local people's priorities, economic circumstances, cultural needs, and with local ecological conditions. They must not impose unfamiliar methods, must be easy to maintain and sustain, and their benefits must be readily visible. Technologies that cannot be easily adopted without vast external cash injections stand little chance of success. It is interesting in this regard that the World Bank ceased to fund large-scale projects and has concentrated instead on rehabilitation of existing projects and small-scale projects, low-cost ventures which can be controlled by the individual farmer or small groups.

With regard to local perspectives, Paul Harrison (1987) argues that it is not true that *only* small-scale projects can succeed while large-scale projects must fail. It is true that large-scale projects with high cost and high risk often do not succeed, but projects which are large-scale in terms of a wide reach or extent *and which adopt appropriate approaches and techniques* can succeed and should be encouraged.

Technological Barriers: A Summary

While technological barriers can be envisaged, quite often the lack of technology is not a barrier in itself. The crucial questions are whether the very existence of technological solutions makes us complacent and whether the technologies are environmentally or socially appropriate.

Complacency certainly exists; we have to overcome the complacency barrier inherent in the 'technological fix' approach by demonstrating the financial and environmental costs of such fixes and that it is cheaper and easier, in the long run, to work with nature than against it.

Inappropriate technologies also certainly exist, and their poor record can act as a barrier to further progress. We have to overcome this by using the criteria of environmental and societal acceptability. These, in turn, can be judged according to whether the technology damages or enhances the life-supporting resource system and whether it can be absorbed by the society in such a way not only that it does not alter its social fabric but also that it enhances it and the quality of life of that society. We thus have to identify people's needs from *their* point of view, rather than from an outsider's point of view, and work with their needs in an environmentally sound way.

Chapter 6

Economic, Social and Political Barriers

Having examined agreement, knowledge and technological barriers, we must now move on to consider barriers of an economic social or political nature. We can illustrate these latter barriers with reference to some of the problems referred to in earlier chapters.

In a study of successes in tackling US soil erosion, Napier (1989) specified 12 necessary, but not sufficient, conditions which must be satisfied, at least to some extent, before soil-conservation programmes can be effectively implemented:

1. A political constituency which supports action to reduce the social, economic and environmental costs of soil erosion.
2. Extensive human and economic resources on a long-term basis to finance soil-conservation programmes.
3. Government agencies commissioned to address soil-erosion problems with sufficient autonomy to be immune from short-term political influences.
4. Well-trained professionals to staff conservation agencies.
5. An informed farm population which is aware of the causes and remedies of soil erosion.
6. Development of a stewardship orientation among land operators to protect soil and water resources.
7. National policies which place high priority on the protection of soil and water resources.
8. The creation of national development, agricultural and soil-conservation policies and programmes which are consistent and complementary.
9. The creation of national environmental policies which are consistent and complementary.
10. The development of physical and social scientists who are committed to the generation of scientific information which will contribute to the creation, implementation and continual modification of soil-and

water-conservation policies and programmes.
11. The creation of an interdisciplinary society committed to the maintenance of environmental integrity of soil and water resources.
12. The emergence of political leadership which will be willing to implement policies and programmes which some segments of the agricultural population will find oppressive.

These conditions mean that as well as some consensus on the problems, goals and solutions there must be adequate understanding of the processes, causes and solutions of the problem in both physical and social terms and their effective communication to those involved. There must also be appropriate problem-solving techniques and economic, administrative and ideological contexts in which to implement the solutions.

In addition, success involves education both at the farmer level and at the political level as well as the training of appropriate scientific personnel with both a physical and social background. The political will to create the appropriate financial conditions for implementation is crucial, especially when the costs of conservation are liable to compare unfavourably with land values and returns to individual farmers. Indeed, Napier notes that:

> *soil conservation is very expensive: individual farmers are seldom motivated to adopt soil conservation practices without being extensively subsidised. The subsidies must be provided by the federal government, since state and local jurisdictions do not have adequate financial resources to address the problem: societies desirous of reducing soil erosion must be prepared to allocate necessary financial and human resources to affect the problem.*

Simply expressed, the factors involved are: goal definition; appropriate and communicated knowledge; appropriate technologies; and appropriate institutional organisation for implementation. Without these, the solution for the individual becomes one of doing very little: only when the higher levels of the goal hierarchy are referred to does a proposal for problem resolution gain acceptance and implementation because of the wider solution scope and feasibility.

We now turn to the problem of ozone depletion. It was clear in Chapter 4 that the problem transcended the boundaries of nations and that international agreement was needed. The primary target for reducing CFCs was aerosol propellants. The United States had already banned the use of CFCs in propellants in 1978, producing 2.5 billion cans of aerosols with alternative propellants by 1985. Canada, Sweden and Denmark have also implemented bans. Now less than 25 per cent of CFCs come from aerosol propellants.

While propellants still remain a cause for concern, once efforts were made to reduce them, the target then shifted to CFCs produced by foam blowing and refrigerators. MacDonald's hamburger chain, the target of a

Friends of the Earth campaign, announced in autumn 1987 that it would shift to foam-blown packages made without CFCs in the following 18 months for use in their 7,600 US restaurants.

On 16 October 1987 an international protocol was signed in Montreal to reduce CFC emissions by 50 per cent of 1986 levels by 1999. This agreement was welcomed by environmentalists, but because CFCs can remain in the atmosphere for centuries it does no more than slow down the depletion of the ozone layer. Environmentalists are also concerned that loopholes exist in the agreement. Third World countries were permitted to increase consumption of CFCs for ten years from the date of the agreement. Also the Soviet Union has yet to sign the agreement on the grounds that its next five year plan is too set to change. There is also the fear that non-signatory countries could also export CFCs back to the developed world.

As a result, global production is expected to *increase* by 15 per cent to 1997 from the agreement date. Thus the effective reduction in output by 1999 will only be 35 per cent rather than the 50 per cent envisaged. It is clear that world opinion had shifted towards acceptance of the case against CFCs but that still further progress needs to be made to achieve a complete and effective ban. The pressure is thus still on for further reductions, especially in view of the longevity of CFCs.

This therefore does not mean that the ozone-depletion problem has been solved; but what is interesting is that once there was a clear acceptance of the problem and *enough* evidence to convince at least some people, and to give environmentalists and pressure groups enough ammunition, thus bringing the problem into the political arena, then action rapidly followed. It is clear that the barriers are now those of loopholes in existing agreements and the reasoning that commitments of industrial development prevent a rapid response.

So perhaps the seeds of success were sown by the development of considerable awareness of the problem and its global implications, aided by wide publicity. It is also clear that a barrier still involves political and industrial inertia rather than any other factor.

Another problem we have considered in earlier chapters is that of nitrate. The health and ecological effects of which are accepted (see Chapter 4). This being so, the question of action arises. There are perhaps two ways to approach this: one is to curb the pollution at source, by restrictions on agriculture; the other is to treat drinking water by denitrification. The problem with the latter is that it does not help with ecological effects. Curbing at source could be by enforced restrictions on fertiliser use and/or by a code of practice to restrict losses concerning timing and placement of fertiliser applications. The latter seen as having only a marginal effect, while the former is often seen as unacceptable in terms of lost productivity and economic viability of individual farmers. Much of this discussion is being overtaken by events, however, and government policies for reducing agricultural production because of surpluses may shift the whole spectrum of the arguments.

The barriers clearly concern causal uncertainty and vested interests. Causal uncertainty rests not so much on absence of evidence for invidual links between fertilisers and eutrophication, but on the relative importance of combined effects from other sources, namely phosphates. The resolution also rests on the nature of the medical evidence.

We turn, finally, to the problem of lead. Given acceptance of its effects (see Chapter 4), it might be thought that problem resolution would have been rapid. However, there are two significant barriers: monitoring intakes and vested interests.

Little effective progress has been made in the matter of lead in food and water. Problems can arise where lead intakes from food alone or from water alone do not give cause for concern in themselves but where the combined lead intakes may exceed the recommended maximum levels. The problems here are that food and water may be analysed separately and both may be near the permitted maximum and that regulations for water and food may be enforced separately. In addition, lead in the air from automobiles has to be taken into account. Because of these multiple sources, the assessment of lead levels in the blood is often seen as the best way of assessing the extent of the problem, rather than the analysis of the different source intakes.

The World Health Organisation's guideline for lead in drinking water is 50 $\mu g\ l^{-1}$. Water authorities can achieve this level by adding calcium hydroxide ($Ca(OH)_2$) which makes lead less soluble and keeps the lead level around 30–40 $\mu g\ l^{-1}$ or below. In 1985, the UK government announced that it intended to meet EC standards on lead in water by 1989, mainly by treating drinking water to make it less acidic; it applied for a delay in applying the standard to the whole country until that time. As an interim precaution, residents of older houses were advised either to run taps first thing in the morning to expel the water lying in the pipes overnight before using water for drinking, or to replace lead pipes.

Problem resolution thus lies in appropriate technology (water treatment) but lack of adequate funding has proved to be a barrier to rapid implementation. Monitoring intake is difficult and monitoring blood is better, but the latter is difficult to implement on a wide scale. In addition, there is inertia in replacing lead pipes if the individual has to bear the cost. The monitoring difficulties can be seen as a barrier of knowledge inappropriateness, and the funding of treatment and replacement as barriers of economic insufficiency.

Effective action has been taken to counter the use of lead weights by anglers. As anglers became aware of the problem, they began substituting them with other weights such as those made of heavy plastic. In July 1985 the UK Junior Environment Minister, Mr William Waldegrave, responded to this situation by announcing the phasing out of lead weights in angling by January 1987.

Thus, although a ban does not remove those weights already existing in the environment, problem resolution came about through a clear problem acceptance. Causal responsibility was accepted, largely through the educated response from anglers who were aware of the problem, and resolution was facilitated by the technological availability of alternatives at no great cost.

Some progress has been made in the drive to reduce the amount of lead in petrol. In 1988 unleaded petrol became cheaper than leaded in the UK when the former was exempted from a rise in duty (giving a price of £1.65 a gallon for unleaded petrol and £1.70 for leaded at the then current prices). This was seen as part of a government policy towards a total conversion to unleaded petrol after 1990.

The slow pace of change was not dictated by the lack of scientific evidence for the detrimental effects of lead – indeed, it is one of the clearest cases which can be made in the field of environmental problems. Rather, it is a story of inertia, especially in terms of investment by industry. The automobile-manufacturing and the petroleum industries see themselves as being unable to change overnight to making cars which run on unleaded petrol and to the national supply of unleaded petrol. Modifications to automobile-manufacturing processes require capital investment and time to implement – in July 1985, Ford UK quoted a figure of £159 million for investment in new developments, and the then British Leyland investment plans were of the order of £1.8 billion. Such levels of investment require careful long-term planning and cannot be easily dropped or changed.

Many UK cars (about 50 per cent) can be converted to run on unleaded petrol at the modest cost of £20. Spurred on by the Campaign for Lead Free Air (CLEAR) and other organisations, government and industrial policy has come more to recognise the growing movement for unleaded petrol. Indeed, demand for unleaded petrol now appears to be rising, even to the extent that people have been reported filling unadapted cars with unleaded petrol. It is clear that the conversion of cars, the production of new engines to run on unleaded petrol and the increased supply of unleaded petrol must be synchronised. In February 1988 unleaded fuel was only available at 715 of the 26 000 petrol stations in the UK. Shell UK, in response to consumer demand, shifts in government policy and to gain recognition from tackling a perceived problem, intended to provide unleaded petrol at 1,000 Shell stations by the end of 1988 – about one-third of all its forecourts – at a cost of some £50 million.

It is thus clear that slow government initiatives, costly investments and time for implementation have all formed barriers. In addition, knowledge barriers were provided by difficulties in monitoring and that contamination of food and water can be monitored and identified more readily, albeit separately, than the more widespread contamination of the atmosphere. The evidence for the links between lead pollution of air, water and food from petrol, industry, lead pipes and lead weights, on the one hand, and human health and wildlife, on the other, is such that the delay in improving this environmental problem was not derived from a lack of scientific research; rather it has come from governmental inertia and vested interests.

Writing in 1986, Brian Price, a freelance pollution consultant and an adviser to Friends of the Earth, said:

> *If one issue can be said to encapsulate all that is wrong with British policy-making, that issue must surely be lead. Official complacency, indifference, dubious scientific reasoning and the power of vested interests are all apparent . . . successive governments have permitted its continued addition to petrol and paint, tolerated its presence in water supplies and ignored the risks which it poses to the health of the nation.*

He continues by saying the benefits from lead use are clear:

> *slightly faster cars, marginally cheaper petrol, a little extra per barrel of oil refined and, in the case of paint, perhaps a slightly cheaper product. But are we, as a society, justified in risking mental health of a significant proportion of our children for these advantages? Clearly we are not.*

He concludes by asking:

> *Can we trust our official watchdogs, in government and civil service, to balance the risks and benefits on our behalf? The answer is again a resounding 'No' since they have signally failed to do so in the sorry history of British lead pollution.*

Thus the barriers seem to be the inertia in political and industrial institutions and the difficulties they face to adapting to new conditions, even when public opinion is clear.

What we learn from the lead issue is that the publication of scientific evidence alone is not enough for action to be taken quickly. Lobbying by pressure groups, the communication of information to the public and the force of public opinion seem to be a prerequisite for changes to be made by industrialists committed in terms of investment and plant and for action by cautious politicians.

The Nature of Economic, Social and Political Barriers

If we are over the hurdles of agreement and knowledge limitations, and we have an appropriate technology for solving a problem, then what is to stop us proceeding to a solution? The answer often lies in economic, social and political barriers. We should therefore now briefly review what we have already said about agreement and knowledge barriers in the context of economic, social and political barriers and then discuss these latter barriers in more detail.

Knowledge is always used – or not used – within political, economic and social frameworks where there are limitations of communication and often a selectivity of purpose. Society often has to be motivated by awareness of a problem in order to apply the relevant knowledge or to promote the relevant research. We have to remember that we live in political systems where there is more kudos to be gained from the demonstrable solution of a disaster than from the avoidance of a possible problem, which is always less tangible. It is often the case that an adverse effect promotes the application of existing knowledge.

While tangible disaster is often a spur to action, the corollary of this is that avoidance of possible problems is often not undertaken. Tangible disaster moves us into the realms of political action. Without it, economic factors and social attitudes are important. People are not likely to take environmentally desirable actions if these costs them money even if they are strongly motivated to do so or they perceive the importance of a long-term gain. On the other hand, if an environmentally desirable action costs no money, then it is likely to be undertaken if an environmental motivation exists. The first barrier is thus often economic; the second, even if an action is not economically detrimental, is social – one of attitudes and motivation. Third in line is political will. This order can be overturned, however, by demonstrable disaster, which can change attitudes and make the necessary money available.

Thus the barriers may change according to the situation; they may also vary according to whether individuals are involved in the actions, when economic and social factors become more dominant, or whether institutions are involved, when political kudos tends to be propelled to the fore. This last point is an important one because many problems are large-scale and multi-faceted and only political institutions have the ability to mobilise the large-scale forces necessary to tackle the issue. Thus, both individual attitudes and corporate attitudes are important factors in solving environmental problems.

In the scientific investigation of our planet we are basically trying to understand the environment, the organisms that live in it (including ourselves) and the ways in which the two are related. Our level of understanding is important not only because knowledge is valued for the way it satisfies our intellectual curiosity concerning the world about us, but also because it forms the basis for creating our environmental management policies. Social, economic and political factors usually determine the actual implementation of management plans, but it is clear that if our understanding of environmental systems is not adequate, then our management plans stand no chance of being adequate.

Quite often, our increased understanding of environmental systems can come from the actual implementation of management plans, that is, when the results of implementation are different from those intended: side-effects and unforeseen reactions then tell us something more than we previously knew about processes and interrelationships. However, the logical basis for future management stems from the prior scientific investigation of the environment simply because it is better to foresee and avoid problems than to improve knowledge at the expense of possible damage to the environment and its resources. In addition, while it is clear that management relates to understanding, it is also clear that the type of understanding relates to the type of scientific investigation. This is especially true in terms of the way we approach scientific investigations in relation to our perception of the environment.

Thus, to ask why we do not solve more environmental problems raises many issues. Clearly, in part the barriers may be scientific, either in terms of lack of knowledge, or because scientists are not necessarily working on the right problems or in the most useful way. But whether or not the scientific knowledge exists, the social context is often the most important. If insufficient knowledge is present, then scientists should look to social priorities to give guidance as to the types of problem that they should work on. If adequate knowledge exists, and it is not being applied (if it is agreed that a problem exists), then the social barriers to implementation should become the focus of attention.

There are thus two priorities for science: first, as we saw in Chapter 4, for physical science to concentrate on clarifying causes and effects; and second, for social science to work on ways of maximising information flow and on the ways in which social factors, such as perception and attitudes, and economic and political factors interact with the scientific knowledge base in the implementation, or lack of implementation, of solutions to perceived problems.

Economic, social and political factors can form substantial barriers between resolution proposal and resolution implementation. These are introduced in Figure 6.1. After initial resolution proposal, prejudices, inertia, vested interests and unacceptable economic, social and political implications give rise to *resolution avoidance.* However, if the resolution is acceptable, the proposal to implement it may again be diverted by these kinds of factors, together with technological inappropriateness, giving rise to initial resolution acceptance but then to *resolution deferral*. After implementation, unacceptable side-effects and/or ineffectiveness can mean that the procedure has to be recycled. The stage we are at, then, is one when problems have been recognised, accepted and resolutions have been proposed. The barriers remaining can be economic, social and political, and can be substantial.

Having briefly reviewed the interactions between the main barriers in general terms, we can now focus on the specific economic barriers.

Economic Barriers

The main factors involved in economic barriers are who pays for tackling a problem – assuming that there is some cost function involved – and who benefits. The answers involve factors of scale, problem causality, time, cost –benefit analysis and economic order (Pearce *et al.*, 1989).

In terms of scale, will the cost be borne locally or at a wider scale? In other words, is the individual going to bear the cost, or will it be borne regionally, nationally or internationally?

Figure 6.1 Stages between resolution proposal and problem resolution. Economic, social and political factors play a major role in avoiding or deferring solutions (shaded).

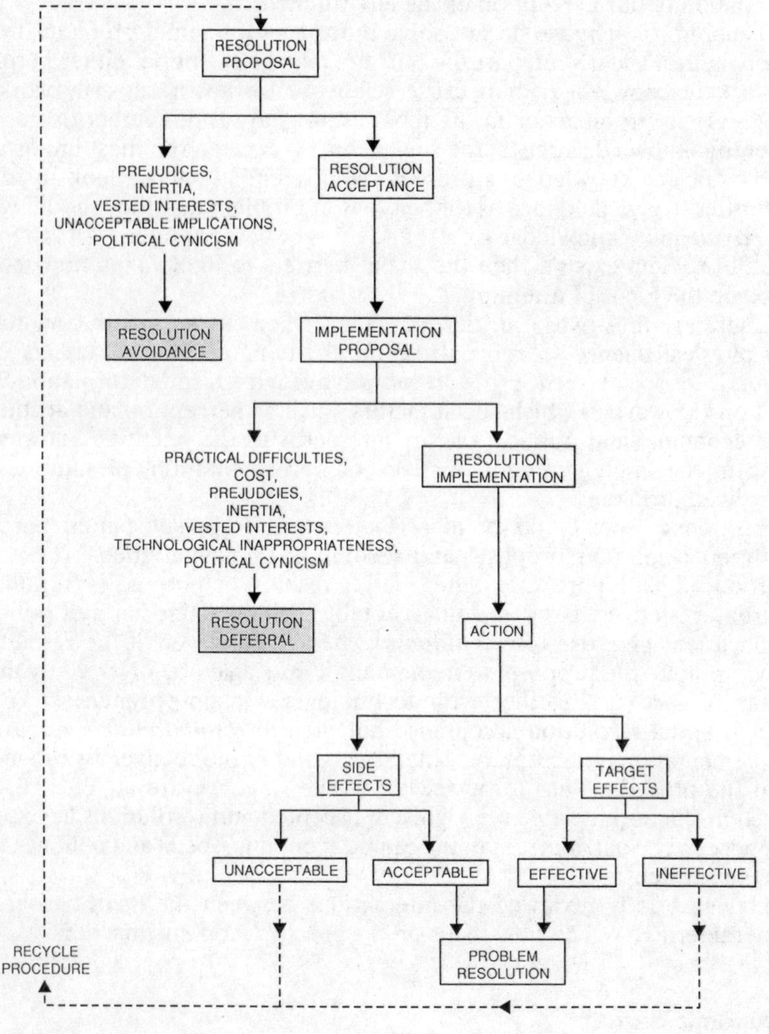

In terms of problem causality, will the cost be borne by the individual or group identified as the cause of the problem (assuming that such identification is possible) or by those who suffer the effects or, indeed, by some intermediary?

In terms of time-scales, will the cost be borne in the immediate short term, or over a much longer term?

In terms of cost–benefit, what is the balance between the costs, including indebtedness, and the benefits which will accrue, and can the benefits be expressed in cash or non-cash terms?

By economic order, we can mean the general national or international economic ethos of a country, which sets the scene for the ways in which costs and benefits are distributed in society. This can mean that there may be a more feudal system where the distribution of benefits is skewed towards a perceived higher order in society, or a more egalitarian system where the benefits are spread more widely in society. It also involves the general nature of economic social organisation, which is often exploitative of resources and which, in ecological terms, can be seen as unsustainable rather than self-sustaining.

Who Pays?

Often, whether the solution is fundamental or limited depends on who is attempting the problem-solving and whether that person has a limited or wide remit. In particular, who is going to pay for any action is important.

Costs for specific actions are liable to be passed on from one production activity to another part of society or *externalised.* For example, the costs of water pollution from a specific industrial activity are often externalised to public utilities such as water authorities rather than internalised by the industry. Externalising costs represents a solution to the industry but not to society as a whole; internalising costs for pollution prevention (the 'polluter pays' principle) represents a more sustainable solution for society if the water resource which is being polluted is also seen as having a value. From the point of view of resource enhancement, it is better for the society to pay for the resource quality via the transfer of the industry's pollution-prevention costs to society by product-pricing strategies, than by the external transfer of costs involving paying water authorities for remedial action on pollution, with the implied intervening resource degradation. In each case the costs might be comparable and they are picked up by society, but in different forms.

The key difference is that internalising costs enhances water-resource conservation while externalising them encourages resource degradation. Remedial action which removes pollutants once they have entered water is an adaptive solution and accepts that pollution is an inevitable consequence of industrial production and economic growth; a more fundamental solution involves the viewpoint that we can have a productive industry without pollution and simply stems from a specific application of general resource-conservation aims.

In addition, there is much discussion over whether it is best to tackle nitrate pollution of water from agriculture by letting farmers use nitrate fertiliser to produce food and then asking water authorities to pay for removing the nitrate – passing their costs onto the consumer (an adaptive solution, accepting the need for agricultural production) – or by employing the more fundamental control solution of minimising fertiliser use in the first place. The latter has the advantage of not paying both to put the fertiliser in the system and to take it out again and of minimising ecological effects as well. It does, however, need addressing at the more radical level of agricultural policy and pricing mechanisms.

These sorts of question are dealt with in some detail by many writers, including Turner (1988) who addresses such important topics as the politics of sustainability and the 'polluter pays' principle, and two important books by Redclift (1984;1987). The question of implementation of fundamental strategies is discussed in detail by Baumol and Dates (1988), who cover both the theory of externalities and the design of environmental policy. In some cases, market forces may prevail, especially when resource scarcity begins to arise and conservation strategies, such as recycling, become more economic, or where information leads to consumer preference and a marketing advantage in 'being green' (as with ozone-friendly deodorants). However, in other cases, intervention may be seen as necessary, for example by taxes or subsidies to achieve cost redistribution. Thus, we can see that achieving cost internalisation is not often easy and naturally meets barriers of vested interests and inertia from industry. In this, and other cases, intervention is liable to be needed to meet overall goals.

This involves both the broad realisation of the need for such policies, and also the political will and public opinion which makes such intervention both economically viable, practically feasible and socially acceptable.

Scale of Cost-Bearing

Understandably, reluctance to bear the cost of any problem-solving exercise comes from those directly involved in paying, and if the cost can be transferred to some other body then willingness to solve the problem by those first involved will increase accordingly. Outside bodies therefore play an important role in problem solution, especially aid agencies, multinational companies, banks and charities. These bodies must, however, go through the steps of problem recognition, problem acceptance, causal clarification and technological appropriateness before they can identify what the problem is an how to tackle it.

In general, such agencies are better at problem recognition and acceptance than many other bodies because they are set up specifically to address themselves to problems. Causal clarification can be uncertain, but again these agencies have a reasonable track record in this area. Technological appropriateness is often more argued over. Many aid agencies are now better at clarifying local needs and funding appropriately than they were and also better than some more financially orientated bodies.

In the case of funding agencies, and with government funding, economic barriers are minimised, but where they are not involved, economic barriers can be severe, especially if the individual has to bear the cost and/or the improvements are seen as luxuries and not necessarily immediate actions to do with survival, productivity and gaining a living. Generally, then, the barriers increase as the scale of cost-bearing decreases, being greater when individuals have to bear the cost and less where groups or corporate bodies are involved.

Causal Liability

This can represent one of the major barriers, both in terms of establishing beyond reasonable doubt where the cause lies and in getting those involved in the cause to pay for improvements. A considerable barrier often exists if only those involved in suffering the effects are involved in bearing the cost.

'The polluter pays' is often seen as a very important principle in tackling environmental problems; it clearly makes sense from a dispassionate point of view and is obviously encouraged by those suffering any damaging effects. However, is the polluter the industry, as many people outside the industry might think, or the users of their industrial product, as the industry might think? It is also often difficult to target a source, especially when many factors are involved in combination. Even if a source can be identified, it is then often difficult to pin down an individual, body or organisation willing to accept responsibility for problem causation and its financial implications. Here, again, problem denial and rejection can occur. For example, electricity generating boards are often seen to play on causal uncertainty in the question of acid rain, pointing out not only that there is sulphuric acid from sulphur dioxide in power-station emissions but also that there are parallel sources of acidity from nitrous oxides in car exhausts which can yield nitric acid. These considerations become important if expensive investment is at issue.

Quite often the source is an unintentional one and is the by-product of some other, quite legitimate, activity. This may also involve productivity and employment, which makes it more difficult to tackle. Thus, for example, getting the agricultural industry to accept responsibility for water pollution from the nitrates in fertiliser is difficult when it is a by-product of a legitimate effort to raise agricultural productivity.

It is perfectly possible, in a technological sense, to have a productive industrial or agricultural system without polluting the environment. However, the reasons why this situation is not necessarily achieved are often to do with cost and the way that pollution prevention can be costly. In fact, pollution-prevention costs may eat into profit margins so that, in order to pay for them, the industry might have to be more productive in order to generate enough financial margin. The other alternatives are to become more orientated towards low-technology so that there is less polluting activity, or to enforce prevention through effective legislation and/or government funding to reduce pollution. Pollution is, of course, a waste and the use of such waste to generate profit could also be a possibility where it is seen that 'pollution is a resource in the wrong place'.

Where pollution is not involved, the situation can be even more difficult to clarify. Should fishermen and whalers pay for research and adequate conservation measures to restock species in decline? Who will pay for the reversal of habitat destruction if, for example, it is the result of tourist development by a diffuse body of individuals? Who bears the cost of birth-control programmes to combat overpopulation? Quite often, the only answer is some corporate one involving governments and international bodies. Getting people to accept responsibility and its financial implications, whether at an individual or corporate level, thus provides a major economic barrier to be overcome.

Time-Scales

This involves the ways in which costs and benefits may be spread over time. A key point is that the benefits to be gained from tackling an accepted problem may not be immediate but only appear in the long term. For example, improvement of water quality and fisheries in eutrophic waters by costly measures to reduce phosphate inputs from sewage and fertiliser restrictions on farmers may only be seen after five or ten years. This is mainly because nutrients already resident in the system will continue to cycle in the system for many years. In such a situation, there can be a reluctance to incur costs when the benefits are seen as only probable and a long way off in the future.

Similarly, there are often benefits to be gained from development, but these are often only short-term. Here, for example, overfishing, overgrazing and the clearance of forests all brought considerable initial economic gains, but because the actions were exploitative, rather than involving husbandry and self-sustainability, they damaged the capacity of the system to renew itself. Careful husbandry would not have brought such great short-term flows of cash but a lower level of long-term benefits would have accrued which would have brought greater overall benefit. As Tim O'Riordan (1976)

Figure 6.2 Time scales of benefits from development and preservation options (adapted from O'Riordan, 1976).

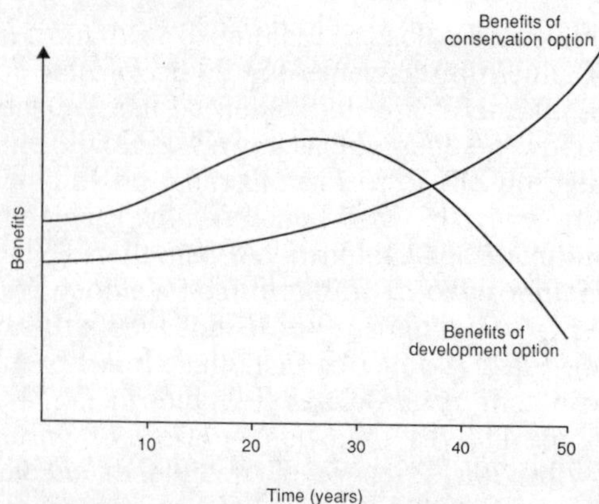

suggests (Figure 6.2) that the benefits of a development option are often considerable but short-lived; the benefits of a conservation option are often initially lower but longer-lasting, and may even increase with time.

This represents a substantial challenge to conventional economics. As highlighted by Pearce *et al.* (1989), a return on the investment is expected as quickly as possible and so investments are normally discounted over a short period of time.

The environmentalist argument arises if there is environmental damage resulting in the long term from, say, resource loss or degradation (for example, nuclear waste disposal or land restoration). If the accounting period is understandably short-term, a conflict arises if costs appear in the long term and are externalised to the accounting of the development enterprise. This then shifts the burden of restoration to future generations. In addition, the actual cost of restoration can be made to appear minimal if the eventual projected costs are discounted back over the life time of the project. Pearce *et al.* (1989) give the example of a radiation hazard due to stored waste costing £1 billion in 50 years' time. Discounting at 5 per cent (the usual Treasury rate) means that the cost in present terms is only £1 000 000 000/$(1.05)^{50}$ or about £87.2 million, one-eleventh of the actual cost at the time of occurrence. When commenting on this apparently low cost in a press release, Friends of the Earth maintained that it 'hardly justifies much expenditure on damage prevention now' and, with short-term accounting leaves future generations to pick up the costs later at the true full cost. The call is for the enterprise to set aside money now which can accumulate interest to pay for the eventual restoration (that is, to invest £87.2 million now at 5 per cent which will amount to £1 billion in 50 years' time). The actual discount rate used also makes a considerable difference, higher rates making the annual costs less and the enterprise more attractive.

In addition, if the benefit is long-term rather than short-term, investment in the future is not financially attractive. In Figure 6.2, if the discounting period is up to 25 years, there will be a substantial return on investment in development (for example, ploughing up land for a return on a crop in a few years), while the conservation option (such as planting trees) yields little benefit. Thus the initial investment in development can be quickly offset by the profit at that time. However, at 50 years, the development option may be running into problems of resource exhaustion, contamination or other costs while the conservation option is paying dividends. People are, however, unwilling to take long-term risks and thus accounting periods are usually short – indeed, often a matter of only a few years.

Since the Brundtland Report (World Commission on Environment and Development, 1987; see Chapter 3 above) defined sustainable development as one that 'meets the needs of the present without compromising the ability of future generations to meet their own needs', it is clear that environmental discounting needs to be longer-term. Then both the long-term benefits of conservation options and the long-term environmental costs of development would be included, rather than just short-term benefits to the long-term detriment of resources. For example, the benefits of nuclear power may be considerable if the investment is discounted over a short period of time; it may not be so attractive if the long-term costs of disposal have to be included in the accounting.

Thus, a considerable barrier to be overcome can be one where short-term economics and development are all that is perceived, rather than long-term benefits.

Cost–Benefit

So far we have talked mainly of costs – over what scale, who is responsible and over what time. But costs have to balanced by the tangible benefits. If such benefits are visible and can be set against costs, then cost implementation is more likely to occur. Such trade-offs can be in money terms or some other non-financial benefit, such as the quality of life or conservation value, but this also raises the question of whether those receiving the benefit are the same as those incurring the cost (discussed under *Economic Order* on p.89). If they are, then implementation is more likely; if not, some degree of altruism has to be involved.

Financial benefits are easiest to assess and cost programmes are most likely to be implemented where they benefit those incurring the costs. Thus, modest soil conservation and agricultural programmes are likely to succeed where the costs are low but the benefits accrue to the farmers involved.

Economic organisation can also be involved here, especially if a soil-conservation and agricultural productivity plan goes hand in hand with an improved marketing scheme. For example, in Zimbabwe, changes since independence in the economic system have brought significant results. Before independence, white farmers had preferential prices for their maize and in 1979 yields were 5–6 tonnes per hectare; black farmers' yields were around only 0.6–0.7 tonnes per hectare. With independence, the prefential pricing system was abolished and new systems of credit, advice, seed types and fertiliser use were instigated. The response was marked, with black farmers' yields increasing to 2.5–4 tonnes per hectare by 1985. The country then had a surplus of around 1 million tonnes for export. Credit arrangements reduced the risk to the individual farmer and the new techniques ensured a good return on capital. Labour shortages were overcome by working collectively, pooling resources to cultivate fields and to harvest the crops. Marketing organisation was crucial to ensure that good prices were obtained for produce and thus the benefits of the agricultural improvement accrued to the individual farmer.

However, if accounting systems are separate, there is less likelihood of a successful implementation. In the UK there is often a confrontation between water authorities and water pollution from agriculture and industry. The polluter has a benefit of not paying to clean up water which is separate from the benefit which the water authority has from paying to clean up water for drinking and there is no overall cost–benefit analysis for industry, agriculture and water together.

Where the benefits are not in financial terms, the cost–benefit analysis is a matter of either assessing the benefits and evaluating them in specific terms or of trying to assess non-financial benefits in financial terms. Thus species diversity, landscape quality and quality of life can be assessed in order to evaluate benefits, though often the difficulty lies in quantifying subjective values on an agreed and recognisable scale. Such procedures are often involved in environmental impact statements (EIAs). For example, an EIA by BP for the Wytch Farm Oilfield development in Dorset, England, considered visual impact, noise, land use, air emissions, effluents, vehicle movement and spillage, which represent a range of factors in terms of ease of assessment and quantification. Visual impact of development was reduced by low-storey buildings, underground installation and tree screening, and a variety of plans where drawn up to assess the visual benefits of alternative schemes.

Assessment of non-financial benefits in financial terms has been promoted by several environmentalists, including Gene Odum from the Institute of Ecology in Athens, Georgia, USA. He has devised ways of quantifying the value of a marsh area in terms of its biodegrading potential for waste and expressed this in equivalent terms of the cost of treatment works which would be need to do the same task. A parallel approach involved the potential real estate value of a view (say, from a standard type of house) and an assessment of the property values which could exist if the landscapes were in different conditions. Such approaches enable benefits – and detriments – to be assessed in financial terms. Thus less tangible benefits are expressed in money terms which 'hard-headed businessmen' can understand. It may be inappropriate to imagine that everything can be expressed in monetary terms because this might deny the aesthetic dimension and intrinsic rights of the environment and its wildlife. However, expressing these dimensions and rights in cash terms may be the only case which developers will accept. It is thus a case of tackling developers in their own terms rather than persuading them by alternative arguments.

Economic Order

On a local or national scale, the economic order constrains who gets the benefit of actions – from the individual through local organisations to the state. On the global scale, we have to consider the way in which finacial rewards can be organised to encourage sustainability rather than exploitation. This is a substantial topic which has recently been tackled in detail by Pearce *et al.* (1989); however, some of the implications of sustainability can be indicated here.

If the individual pays for a programme and benefits from it directly, then this represents a viable proposition. An example might be on-site developments on farms where conservation areas are set aside and then charges are made for visitors to enjoy such areas. Similarly, a farmer planting hedges may benefit from increased productivity due to the shelter they provide. In areas prone to soil erosion and where there are shortages of fuelwood, similar benefits may accrue from tree planting such as alley cropping, the trees acting to minimise downslope movement of soil, providing fodder for cattle and providing a renewable source of fuelwood from thinnings and without harming indigenous vegetation.

On a wider scale, it is clear that exploitation pays, at least in the short term. This applies to situations involving manufacturing, where obsolescence promotes continued sales – at the expense of resources. This is often a situation encouraged by larger companies, especially, and understandably, where the potential profits are clear. It also exists in issues like forest clearance, where the initial benefit to individuals or corporate bodies can be large. What is clear, however, is that such development is unsustainable in the long term, as we have already discussed. From an ecological point of view, such unsustainability is clearly short-sighted but we have to understand that short-term economics tends to dominate, especially from the point of view of an individual who has an immediate context of survival to deal with.

Self-sustainability is not only ecologically sensible, it will also promote a sounder, sustained economic development in the long term, as stressed by the Brundtland Report. However, the Report's recommendations depend upon increases in per capita income in the Third World in order to be able to deal with threats to people and the biosphere. This may not be particularly realistic, and the Commission does not provide details of how it might be acheived. A crucial question is whether sustainable policies can work if they have to be slotted into the present unsustainable economic order – or whether the economic order itself has to changed. If the latter, what prospects are there of changing it? At this level, the solution involves recognition of longer-term benefits and interim support till the benefits accrue.

It is most probable that we will evolve to a more ecologically sound, self-sustainable economic order as the gradual realisation comes that environmental quality and economic viability are closely linked. For example, in India, prompted by the work of the Centre for Science and Environment in Delhi, it is becoming realised that the environment is not a luxury, to be 'fitted in' after development in an order of priorities, and that exploitative development must stop because it leads to land degradation and poverty. Forest cover and soil conservation need to be promoted in order to sustain the agricultural base and to safeguard water supplies so that economic viability can be promoted.

Economic Barriers: Summary

Economic barriers can thus be seen to exist:

(1) when costs have to be borne by individuals or groups unable to see an immediate cash benefit – an *economic insufficiency* barrier.
(2) where such individuals or groups accept neither the responsibility for causing problems nor the financial implications of such an acceptance

– either because of causal uncertainty or because of problem denial or rejection due to vested interests – an *economic denial* barrier.

(3) where short-term considerations dominate – an *economic inappropriateness* barrier.

(4) where the economic order is exploitative – especially where the perceived situation is one of individuals struggling for survival and immediate, tangible benefit or where the profits of companies are at stake – an *economic exploitation* barrier.

These barriers can be tackled by:

(1) maximising cash benefits and stressing the importance of long-term benefits as well as quantifying and/or pointing out the value of non-cash benefits.

(2) directing scientific research to minimising causal uncertainty, and tackling denial and rejection by pointing out responsibility. This latter point can be achieved most effectively by increasing the status and kudos accruing from tackling a problem in the context of a social climate where such things are sought and recognised as worthy; by recognising that cash benefits can accrue from such actions and can offset costs in many cases; and by improving accounting systems so that vested interests are not so separate and opposable but are rationalised in a more overall manner.

(3) pointing out the inadequacy of the short-term viewpoint, both in terms of tackling existing problems and in terms of new developments. Long-term viewpoints stress that conservation benefits are liable to be greater than short-term exploitative benefits.

(4) changing the present unsustainable economic order, not by rapid or violent means, which would lead to disruption and opposition, but by an evolution where it is pointed out and realised that a high-quality environment and a viable economy not only are compatible but also in fact have common objectives of self-sustainability and thus go hand-in-hand with each other, as discussed by Pearce *et al.* (1989).

During the discussion of economic barriers, it has become apparent that many of the barriers relate not only to money but also to the ways in which society is organised and governed. These factors should therefore now be considered.

Social Barriers

The Nature of Social Barriers

Social barriers are obviously closely interlinked with economic and political ones, but they are sufficiently distinct to merit separate consideration. Here, we shall discuss how the ways in which society is organised and holds value systems can have considerable impact on environmental problem-solving. However, it should be stressed at the outset that no single form of social organisation can provide the ideal way of promoting environmental problem-solving; some highly organised, centralised authorities might be seen to have the power to direct and implement problem-solving while more diffuse, less organised societies may be less able to do so but may be more in touch with the land and, with their more intimate involvement with their environment, may be more attuned to a successful relation with it. There are many ways of organising society and many different value systems, with no single universal formula or recipe for success.

The important aspects of social organisation and value systems which are involved include the ways in which environmental problem-solving relates to:

(1) the general perceptions, beliefs, value systems and the consequent practices of the society;
(2) the ideology of the society, for example whether it is Marxist or capitalist, democratic or authoritarian;
(3) the social structure in terms of whether it is more centralised or diffuse and more hierachical or egalitarian, especially in relation to land tenure;
(4) the ways in which society is organised in terms of decision-making and where real power lies, and especially whether the society has a centralised body for environmental decision-making or not and whether protest groups are effective in influencing such decisions;
(5) the changes which may be made to the social fabric, whether these will damage or enhance the fabric, and, indeed, how such changes are to be assessed and evaluated.

Many of these relate closely to political power, which will be discussed in the next section. Here, we shall focus on the social organisation aspects of these topics and we can divide our discussion into two main topics – value systems and organisation – though these are often intermixed. However, we can suggest initially that the specific barriers involved are the value-system barriers, which relate very closely to the agreement barriers we discussed in Chapter 3, and the organisational barriers which involve the way in which resources, especially land, are held by different people and what they are free or constrained to do with them. Thus, social attitudes and social organisation form the two major topics of this section.

Social Attitudes to Environmental Problems

The attitudes inherent in a society are crucial to environmental problem-solving. There is, first, the question of how people value a resource or environment, whether in a utilitarian or aesthetic sense. This involves some fundamental attitudes to the environment and whether they are spiritual, with a sense of personal responsibility, or whether responsibility is transferred to some other body, organisation or government.

Attitudes also involve whether people actually see a problem and its significance, as we suggested in Chapter 3. This involves not only the ways in which people communicate, but also, and perhaps more importantly, the ways in which they use information in society in terms of the significance placed on the information.

A major barrier is also provided by the ways in which people perceive proposed changes, from both the inside and the outside. The questions here are whether there is a perceived social benefit or not, whether the implementation of an environmental programme involves social change or not and, if it does, whether it is right to alter a society, even if the change is thought to be for the better. This, in turn, involves judgement as to what is thought to be 'better' and a question of the perception of local needs by outsiders as much as of the perception of ecologically desirable actions by all concerned.

A spiritual relationship with the environment

Earlier, in Chapter 3, we made the point that less centralised, diffuse societies are likely to be in closer harmony with their environment. One thinks here of the North American Indians, the African Bushmen, the Australian Aborigines, the Amazonian Indians and many other so-called 'primitive' people who in fact had, or still have, a very advanced, detailed, sympathetic and mutually beneficial relationship with their environment. Many of these relationships have been lost during the course of so-called 'progress' and 'civilisation' whereby so many of us have become detached from an immediacy with the environment.

In this context, we can refer again to Laurens van der Post's writings on the Kalahari bushmen and their intimacy with their surroundings. Van der Post records how the bushmen could survive in conditions where most 'civilised' people would perish and in a way that meant they were well nourished and healthy and how they in no way damaged or exploited their environment. In *A Far-off Place* (1974) he writes about the troubles which afflict modern man:

> *Statesmen, scientists, philosophers, even priests and the whole intellectual trend of the day put up a plausible pretence that our troubles were due to imperfect political systems, badly drawn frontiers and other environmental and economic causes. The whole history of man . . . had tried all those approaches over and over again and at last . . . they were proved utterly bankrupt. The real, the only crisis out of which all evil came was a crisis of meaning. It was a terrible invasion of meaninglessness and a feeling of not belonging invading the awareness of man, that was the unique sickness of the day. And*

> *this sickness . . . was a result of the so-called civilised man, parting company with the natural and instinctive man in himself. Never had the power of the civilised over the natural been so great and never had the power corrupted man . . . so dangerously. . . .*
>
> *The journey to total reconciliation within depended on man standing fast at last in his surroundings and there refusing to give way to any assault on his integrity. [The important way ahead was by] accepting what was nearest at hand and working through it out of love in the most imaginative, precise and intimate co-operation with nature around and within . . . man.*

I have quoted this at length because it seems to sum up the importance of a close relationship with the environment, as much for the sake of the spiritual being of mankind as for the sake of the environment. It is also interesting in our context because it focuses on individual attitudes held in society as more important in a problem-solving context than those of some distant 'them' to which our troubles are often referred. Indeed, the implication of this is that to start problem-solving one does not necessarily have to refer to corporate bodies as the first stage, but instead to attempt to redress a spiritual impoverishment found in individuals in society. But how practical is this?

We can see that some 'primitive' societies are certainly much closer and more attuned to the environment than other 'advanced' societies, but to return to some primeval state on a global scale is not usually seen as a viable alternative to solving our problems – and we have to start from where we are rather than from where we might be. The way must be to attempt to retain that which is good about our civilised society while adopting a set of values appropriate to being in tune with nature. *It must be possible to have material possesions, transport systems, energy, food and recreation while also having a caring, non-exploitative, self-sustainable approach to the environment.* For many of us, isolated in cities from direct contact with the environment, except during leisure periods, such an approach must necessarily be developed second-hand and here television nature programmes have been important in promoting such a caring attitude.

Another encouragement recently has been the growth of Earth Education or 'Acclimatisation' as promoted by Steve van Matre from America. This places a high priority on involvement with the environment during education, especially by the development of tactile, visual and auditive skills through primary experience in the field. This approach has been widely adopted and has a high profile in field education in the UK through such bodies as the National Parks and the Field Studies Council. It has been responsible for the awakening of a sense of wonder, care, responsibility and of being rather than having or doing and thus for redressing some of the spiritual impoverishment which van der Post lamented, but there is still a long way to go.

We can conclude that, not without a touch of whimsy and nostalgia, the lack of close involvement with the environment – an involvement such as our early ancestors had and the more 'primitive' peoples of the earth still have – lies at the root of many of our problems. This represents a considerable social attitude barrier to be overcome, but education of attitudes, especially through attractive and exciting television programmes and through Earth Education programmes, points the way ahead.

A slight reserve is sometimes expressed by those who see attitude education as a form of indoctrination, and that 'we know best' and you have 'got to think like this' are involved. An answer to this criticism comes from the saying that 'you can't teach anybody anything, only help them learn'. A cliché perhaps, but one with a good deal of truth in it. Thus, provision of opportunities for children to find out what they want for themselves is a crucial aspect of this. In addition, as any educationalist will tell you, and at the risk of introducing another cliché, 'you can take a horse to the water, but you can't make it drink' – by which I mean to imply that it is probably unfair to label attitude education as indoctrination. It is also arguable that many environmental problems are so pressing, because they threaten our life-support system in so many ways, that such education is extremely vital.

Communication and use of information

Social attitudes are again important in the way in which information is used, as we have already seen when discussing agreement barriers. Information can be readily rejected as irrelevant or innapropriate if it does not relate to the value system of the society concerned, or, indeed, if it is presented in in unclear, jargonised and complicated fashion. We have invented some jargon already when talking of problem denial and rejection but, putting it more simply, it is a matter of when information is available but *people just don't see it* – it doesn't have any impact or relate to them and their conditions or other reference points.

There is thus a selectivity involved in information use and it may just not mean anything to people when they are told that what they are doing is causing a problem. Thus, overcoming this information-selectivity barrier is a matter of presenting the information in an appropriate manner and making it relevant by looking first at people's actual needs, rather than by imposing outside information. Many of the aid agencies are getting rather better at this, but it is still something of a lesson which could be more universally learned and applies equally whether you are addressing a multinational company or a starving Third World society.

Learning by example and demonstration remain crucial aspects of communication, especially if people are to see how a practice could be beneficial to them. There is a saying in educational circles: 'Tell me, I forget; show me, I remember; involve me, I understand.' Involving people in the demonstration of tangible benefits is an important step and rather more effective, and less presumptively arrogant, than visiting experts telling people what to do.

Learning by example is an approach supported by Paul Harrison (1987), who talks of the value of projects which have appropriate approaches and techniques and which are large-scale in terms of a reach or extent. These can succeed and should be encouraged and spread by example. Governments can play as important a part in their spread as voluntary organisations. Harrison writes about the spread of appropriate projects in Africa: He does not '*pretend that the battle is well on the way to being won. . . . the breakthroughs are surrounded and vastly outnumbered by the failures . . . but . . . success stories are like seeds. If they are sown widely enough, they can take over the field.*' What we have to do is to '*try to extract the secrets of their success*' and thus to encourage the spread of successful projects.

Thus, social communication barriers involve two related things. The first concerns the relevance of the information to those concerned. The second involves the way in which it is communicated. Barriers arise when the information is seen as irrelevant, but these can be overcome when it is put over in an appropriate fashion, which involves peoples' participation and addresses their needs, so that the relevance of the information can be demonstrated.

The morality of inducing social change

Social change is a minefield of dissension, not least because people have been trying to change society ever since society began. Some people, out of profound conviction, try to alter the rest of society, by argument or by force, to fit in with a scheme which they perceive to be better; others argue that societies are sacrosanct and should be left alone in their integrity and not be interfered with.

Thus, anyone entering this area of discussion has to tread carefully, lest accusations of social engineering, revolution, arch-conservatism, preservation and the like should be thrown in the face of any proposal. Yet the issues have to be squarely faced – issues such as poverty in relation to environmental degradation should be tackled if we are to be thought of as a caring world community. While many approaches to change are possible, a convincing persuasion, with ample discussion of alternative points of view, is probably the most dignified approach to adopt.

Confrontation is more likely if entrenched attitudes against change meet profound conviction about the need for change. The hope is that the 'civilised' label attached to our modern society refers to the civilised ability to agree on the need for change, on goals and on mechanisms, though discussion and negotiation rather than by confrontation. However, as Jonathon Porritt (1988) of Friends of the Earth has said: '*You have to remember that for every friend of the earth there are at least as many enemies. So I am afraid you would find in me a deep grain of confrontation*' (quoted in Trudgill, 1988). This is a realistic approach, but again we can look to education, both at school and of adults, to decrease this confrontation in the future, especially by demonstrating the common interest we all have in a self-sustained planetary system.

What we have to avoid is a situation where environmentalists set themselves up as somehow 'knowing better' promoting instead a situation where they *facilitate* others coming to environmentally sound conclusions about the ways in which society could approach its organisation, values and relationships with nature; by 'environmentally sound', I mean where the resource system and its life-support ability are not damaged but sustained. This applies especially to approaches to changing society. Nothing moves so fast as a society which wants to change – as opposed to a society which is being told to change from outside. Thus, the important thing is to point out the alternatives and the consequences of adopting different options. Producers of goods are very responsive to consumer demand and consumer awareness is an important part of change; if consumers perceive that a product is better for them and less environmentally damaging, producers will respond appropriately and in a way which will tend to bring prices down because of increased production. Peasant farmers will tend to adopt practices if they perceive the advantages; the important thing is to point out that while some options may have immediate advantages, often in cash terms, others may have greater long-term advantages because they do not damage the resource on which they depend – and also to demonstrate that this long-term, environmentally sound option exists and that it matters.

If this can be done, then the question remains of preserving and enhancing the social fabric of that society. The overall goal is that it must be possible to implement environmentally sound policies while conserving the fabric of the society involved. Such policy implementation does not mean that the society has to be changed by regimentation, social engineering, revolution or other means. It is important to be able to implement environmentally sound policies in all sorts of societies because there is a far greater chance of success if such policies can be adapted to differing conditions than if they involve doctrinaire statements of universal behaviour. So we do not necessarily have to change societies to improve the environment, indeed, so many problems faced by some societies are a result of environmental degradation that many will be enhanced by environmental improvement. We also have to ask why we want to improve the environment. The answers in part revolve around the intrinsic value of the environment in its own right but, in many ways, it is in our own long-term self-interest to improve the environment. This means that we should have a good chance of implementing improvements in a very wide range of societies.

This is not to say that there is not a core of requirements which environmental programmes have to have – there is, and self-sustainability is obviously one of them. Neither is it to say that conflicts about changing society cannot arise – they can, but they have to be met in terms of evaluation of alternatives and their consequences. Birth control to tackle overpopulation is one example where value systems, customs, practices and expectations are involved. The alternatives to birth control are overpopulation and resource exhaustion. Here again, it is important to address peoples' self-identified needs: many people have large families because they sense an insecurity about the life expectation of children. Improve that security with effective health care and many will adopt birth control of their own accord. This is not always the case, of course, and religious beliefs and factors like the perceived need for a son and heir are also important. But a socially sensitive programme which integrates environmentally sensible policies with peoples' needs facilitates the enhancement of a society rather than imposing on it.

We can conclude that many social barriers to change come from the many attitudes inherent in a society, but that, once identified, it is not so much a matter of overthrowing them as of recognising them and then working with them towards environmentally sensible goals which will sustain the resource base and meet peoples' perceived needs. The goal can thus be that the fabric of a society can be enhanced by realising that environmentally sensible programmes can be integrated into a society and that this can be achieved by demonstrating the benefits of such programmes which then facilitates implementation by people's own volition and conviction. Thus, this is not the imposition of missionary zeal, to convert people to an ecological way of life by dictation, but a demonstration of consequences and benefits so that they can retain their own dignity and enhance their self-esteem though a self-motivated and self-sustaining, productive and mutually beneficial relationship with the environment.

Social Organisation

While the attitudes of individuals and groups in society are crucial, social structures and organisation, whether formal or informal, can be equally important. Many people who wish to tackle environmental problems have to recognise that such structures can be the cause of problems and that they have to be understood and worked with if the problems are to be tackled. Especially important are the decision-making structures and the evaluation of who is able to do what and who is constrained by some higher authority. The existence of 'refereeing' organisations and of pressure groups are also significant factors. The structure of land-ownership organisation is also a vital consideration in many environmental problems.

Environment programmes can easily founder if the appropriate community leaders are not adequately identified and their involvement is not sought. This may simply be the head man in the village or religious figures in the community, government officials, agricultural extension officers or whoever people look up to in the society. In addition, it is inadequate simply to address local people if real authority comes from somewhere up the hierarchy, say in a more distant town or city. Officials of whatever kind can be conservative in attitude and resent challenges to their authority, however well intentioned.

Thus, a considerable barrier can exist if the inappropriate people in the society are addressed and, even if the appropriate people are identified and involved, there can then be resistance to implementation because of vested interests within the social structure.

Government organisation and the way in which governments listen, or do not listen, to environmental views can be a vital consideration. In some countries a central body exists to 'referee' environmental decision-making, such as the Environmental Protection Agency (EPA) of the United States. Such bodies can be important in overcoming barriers if they are given effective powers by governments. Then they can collate and evaluate differing viewpoints and make policy representations to governments.

Charles Secret, Friends of the Earth campaign organiser, told me in 1988 that he thought that one of the biggest barriers to tackling environmental problems in the UK was the lack of such a central body. You have to address so many organisations and individuals to get anywhere, including the Department of the Environment, other ministries, Members of Parliament, and non-governmental organisations.

This is not to say that the mere existence of a central body would automatically lead to easier solutions; the body would have to have both credibility and effective powers to be of use. Without such a body, or even with one, pressure groups can be very effective in relation to influencing public opinion. It has been noticeable how groups like Friends of the Earth and Greenpeace have been given greater credence by UK society in recent years through media coverage of their views and activities.

The role of government policy in causing and tackling problems is illustrated in John Clarke's (undated) book, *Ethiopia's Campaign against Famine*. Clarke charts the policies of earlier governments in relation to land tenure as a prime instigator of environmental degradation and famine. This is also supported by Dessalegn Rahmato (1985). Landlordism, whereby the benefits of cultivation were transferred to landlords, subdivision of plots and pressures for cultivation on steep slopes are seen as the prime cause of soil erosion and the loss of the ability of agriculture to sustain itself in earlier years.

The current government has recognised these problems and transferred all rural land to public ownership so that independent peasant production occurs and the farmer gains the benefit of production – notwithstanding the fact that those critical of Ethiopia have pointed out that the country exports some foodstuffs while some of its people starve. Taking the point of view that environmental degradation had reached crisis proportions in the North, government resettlement programmes were instigated to resettle people from the North in the more fertile and productive areas in the West.

This programme was controversial because it involved the wholesale movement of people, according to critics, against their will. However, Clarke's view is that they moved willingly because of environmental degradation in their homelands. The important thing also was that coercion was not involved, simply the provision of information, opportunity and facilities to promote the self-motivation of the people involved. While people have argued over the merits of the government policies and their ideological basis, the clear characteristics of improvement were land reform – giving the land, and its products, to those who farmed it – and a socially sympathetic process which encouraged self-motivation rather than imposition.

We can conclude, therefore, that organisation can exercise considerable influence on problem-solving. First, if outsiders involved in implementation do not identify and involve community leaders, they will be less successful than if they do. Government policies are also crucial and can be influenced by organisations set up to evaluate environmental policies and by pressure groups. Finally, governments can be very effective in implementing policies such as land reform if they so wish and are indeed the only organisational level really able to implement such overall policies.

The Social Determinants of Soil Erosion

It is already clear, from the US example discussed at the beginning of this Chapter, that sociological factors are a crucial determinant of erosion and the success of conservation programmes. In order further to illustrate and clarify the social barriers to solving environmental problems, we can extend our earlier discussion to include examples of soil erosion in Third World countries.

Soil is a crucial resource used by people and a vital component of environmental systems. The erosion of soil represents a loss of self-sustainability of the life-support resource base and thus a serious threat to the continued welfare of people in many countries.

Many physical scientists have undertaken a considerable amount of research on the processes of soil erosion which has lead to the formulation of conservation measures aimed at minimising soil erosion. Thus, we have a good grasp of the processes involved and of the technical solutions to the problem. Yet soil erosion still occurs throughout the world.

The barriers to minimising soil erosion are, in fact, largely economic, social and political. Thus, in an important book, Blaikie (1985) has written on the political economy of soil erosion in developing countries. There is very little discussion of the physical mechanics of erosion. Assuming that if steep slopes are cultivated, then soil erosion is liable to occur, the more fundamental causes of such cultivation are discussed; among these are population pressures, local political strategies, social structures and economic pressures. This kind of social context was never contemplated by earlier works on erosion and conservation such as that by Hudson (1971), notwithstanding its extremely sound coverage of the physical processes involved in erosion and its excellent treatment of conservation measures.

Reinforcement of the importance of the sociological context comes from a key research paper by Blaut *et al.* (1959) on the cultural determinants of soil erosion in the Blue Mountains in Jamaica. The authors chart the failure of initial soil-conservation measures which did not take into account sociological factors and the subsequent sucesses of of their adoption once a sociologically sensitive plan had been devised. The documentation of the case study shows that perceptions and land tenure were vital components, as were leadership in the community and security of livelihood.

Initial attempts at soil conservation were sociologically inept because the role of community leaders and of social attitudes were not allowed for. Visiting experts were involved in soil-conservation promotion and inappropriate technologies were proposed. The lack of perception that soil erosion was a problem formed a significant barrier. Soil erosion was thought of as natural, rather than man-made, and therefore not capable of solution. Success came through involving community leaders and the education of key people in the community. They, rather than outsiders, then acted to communicate the important ideas. The peasant economy was enhanced by the promotion of cash crops, but ones which were not produced by means which encouraged soil erosion. Soil-conservation measures were simply, cheaply and easily maintained and renewed by local people without outside technical or financial assistance. A crucial step was the reform of land tenure when, rather than working for landlords, people were working for themselves and taking more care of the land, especially by planting trees which show mainly long-term benefits. The social structure was evaluated, especially the importance of women going to markets to support families, and this was encouraged by the growing of appropriate marketable produce. The lessons of this project could be more widely applied.

Social Barriers: A Summary

Many environmental problems are socially determined and thus can only be tackled by addressing social issues. In parallel, environmental degradation can cause social distress. Thus, tackling social and environmental problems in an integrated fashion is an important process.

Social barriers involve resistance to new ideas because of perceptions, beliefs and values; inadequate identification of community hierachies and leadership; dilemmas over the morality of induced social change; a diffuseness of the decision-making process and problems of land tenure, especially where people do not reap the rewards of their own efforts.

Many of these social barriers can be addressed by education. Education of values is difficult but possible. Communication of ideas in an effective and relevant manner is crucial and demonstration is an effective form of education. Care has to be taken to enhance a society in a way that meets its own perceived needs, rather than changing it according to outside ideas. Land reform is an essential factor in social organisation and promotes a motivation for husbandry rather than exploitation. Environmentally sensible programmes and social enhancement are not incompatible and, indeed, go hand in hand.

Political Barriers

Political Motivation

Governments, regional councils and local councils often display a certain inertia in the implementation of policies. Yet, having chosen to implement a policy, they can be most effective in this because of their wide powers. It is thus important to try to understand the motivation of governments and councils rather than just blaming them for inaction.

First, it is important to stress that any form of government can be involved in creating and perpetuating environmental problems, whether socialist or capitalist, authoritarian or democratic – each can be just as exploitative.

Second, it is clear that political motivation comes from a perceived practical or ideological advantage from the point of view of the political institution, whether it be in terms of votes or in terms of reinforcing or demonstrating the value system or ideology of the institution. So politicians may not act either because they do not believe in the tenets underlying the action or because they do not see any political advantage in an action – a curious mixture of somewhat cynical pragmatism and idealism.

Thus, it becomes necessary to show not only the wisdom of a course of action in idealistic environmental terms but also the potential political advantages of such action, whether it be in terms of votes or of reinforcement of ideology.

Evolution or Revolution

This is assuming that we are working within current political frameworks, rather than overthrowing them. It is true that many see the way ahead in terms of replacing current frameworks, but it is also evident that working within current frameworks is more likely to succeed because existing political institutions can then adopt environmental policies without feeling that their basis is threatened.

The existence of a green party can be interesting in this context, because while it proposes to replace existing systems with another, more ecological system, one of its main effects can be to make other parties vie for acclaim by proposing that they, too, have green policies.

Thus it is important to involve all shades of government – socialist or capitalist, authoritarian or democratic – in green politics rather than necessarily replacing existing government by a green government, though the existence of a green party can be very instrumental in this. This is a separate issue from dissention over political ideology, which is highly unlikely ever to be resolved with universal acclaim. Realism suggests that it is more useful to adapt and adopt green policies from within existing frameworks as a strategy which is more likely to be effective and more widely acceptable than replacement – green evolution rather than revolution.

This is not to say that one should not lose sight of the ideal of green governments because such a development would promote planetary self-sustainability and because such an ideal is instrumental in the greening of existing institutions. It is more like a pragmatic first step. This is important because when one listens to green politicians, it is often difficult to disagree with their beliefs and goals – things like harmony, peace and self-sustainability. But it is often very difficult to see how they propose to get from where we are now to where they aim to be. Thus, we have initially to work within current frameworks – and more will follow through education and development of appropriate value systems – but without losing sight of ultimate ideals by saying that we can only work within current systems in a defeatist sense.

Political Advantages

What, then, are the political advantages of environmental problem-solving? This is a crucial question because if there are no answers, it is little wonder that we do not solve environmental problems as we exist in societies which are often dominated by political systems. The lack of a political advantage can thus provide a major barrier to environmental problem-solving. This is especially true when one concedes that politics is an insecure business and that a party or regime can be overthrown or at least challenged if unpopular measures are proposed.

The specific barriers can be seen as a lack of vote-catching potential in a policy or action, simply because people do not see any self-interested advantage in that policy or action and a lack of belief that a policy matters – especially if it is seen as less important than the implementation of some other policy such as one that tackles unemployment or promotes a political ideology such as nationalisation or free-market enterprise. Clearly, overcoming these barriers involves the promotion of the points of view that there are votes in environmental policies, via the route of education and public opinion, and that environmental policies matter and are not inimical to other policies and can indeed promote social well-being rather than detract from it.

It is also true that political advantage can come from the demonstrable solution of a crisis or problem, rather than from the prevention of a possible problem. This may mean that many problems will not be tackled until they have reached sufficient proportions to have an impact on the consciousness of the public, politicians and government. This again means that information and awareness can be crucial precursors of actions, especially information about situations, evaluations of their desirability and the consequences of alternative options for action and inaction. Thus, there is a certain inertia to be overcome and a need for the demonstration of the nature and significance of a problem before action is likely to be taken by the appropriate individual or group of people.

The Scale of Problem Referral

This raises the question of where you have to go in the political system to solve a problem. Obviously, this depends in part on the scope of the problem: some local issues need only to be referred to local councils to be resolved; others are a matter of national policy; still others, like air pollution, clearly need to be referred to the international scale. Thus, the scope of the problem is a determinant of the scale to which it is necessary to go.

On the other hand, the structure of the decision-making hierarchy may make it necessary to go beyond what might at first have seemed to be the appropriate scale. Thus, if a local problem cannot be resolved locally, a more regional or national approach might be more effective. Similarly, if action at a national scale is appropriate but lacking, it may then be necessary to refer to a more international scale to bring in effective action. Thus the scale of referral may well be one or two steps above that which might be initially thought to be appropriate.

Political Barriers: A Summary

It is clear that in many cases, for those in power, power itself is a primary consideration; environmental considerations tend to be secondary. However, power can be enhanced through environmental, and thus social, improvements. We have thus taken the point of view that those in power will be encouraged to take action when they can see some practical or ideological advantage in doing so. Barriers to implementation exist if they do not and thus the task of overcoming them involves the realisation that they exist and then emphasising the advantages of overcoming them. A significant difficulty in this lies in the fact that many advantages are often long-term, rather than immediate, and that political life is essentially insecure. We have to realise this and work with the situation. Demonstration of problems and their significance forms an important step in overcoming this situation because political advantage can be gained from the demonstrable solution of a perceived problem, especially when social and political enhancement can be achieved by solution implementation.

In this brief discussion of political barriers, (for further discussion, see Johnston, 1989) we have moved towards a more pragmatic discussion of real world processes. Thus, having discussed the major barriers in general, it will now be appropriate to turn to problem-solving in the real world.

Chapter 7
Overcoming the Barriers

In Chapters 2–6, we discussed a number of barriers which may exist to finding and implementing solutions to environmental problems. In this chapter we summarise these and look at examples of specific problems, discussing the identification of barriers in each case. Then we discuss how they might be overcome and conclude with an agenda for action.

Summary of the Barriers

The first questions (Table 7.1 (a)) concerned what constituted a problem and the motivation to solve problems, which we defined as situations which damaged the resource base of the planet and its life-support system. Motivation for tackling a problem then comes from our moral obligation and our self-interest in enhancing the resource base and its life – thus enhancing, rather than destroying, planetary ecosystems and plant and animal species, including ourselves. If such motivation exists, or if it is lacking but the motivation barrier can be overcome, then we turn to barriers to solution and implementation, as listed in Table 7.1 (b).

These barriers do not necessarily follow each other in strict sequence, and while there is a tendency for them to do so, some barriers, like economic and social ones, can appear earlier in the sequence. We can suggest, however, a systematic sequence of environmental problem-solving into which problems can be fitted, as shown in Figure 7.1. This progresses from situation recognition through problem recognition and acceptance to resolution proposal, acceptance and implementation and problem resolution. At each stage, there are critical evaluations (1–7). These are concerned with available information, perspectives, problem significance, causal uncertainty, implications of resolution proposal, and desirability and effectiveness of the resolution. The evaluations either allow the progression to proceed or, if there is a negative evaluation, the progression is halted in states of situation uncertainty or refutation, problem denial, rejection, or dismissal or resolution avoidence or deferral. If these exist, the task of the

Table 7.1. Barriers to environmental problem-solving: a summary

(a) MOTIVATION

What is a problem?
Why should we bother with it?

(b) BARRIERS TO SOLUTION AND IMPLEMENTATION

1. AGREEMENT
Situation uncertainty
Situation recognition but problem denial
Problem recognition but problem rejection
Problem acceptance but causal uncertainty
Problem dismissal

2. KNOWLEDGE
Knowledge inadequacy
Knowledge adequacy but knowledge rejection
Knowledge adequacy but knowledge inappropriateness
Knowledge adequacy but knowledge uncommunicated

3. TECHNOLOGICAL
Technological unavailability
Technological availability but technological complacency
Technological availability but technological inappropriateness

4. ECONOMIC
Economic insufficiency
Economic denial
Economic inappropriateness
Economic exploitation

5. SOCIAL
Social value systems
Social resistance
Social leadership
Social allocation
Social morality

6. POLITICAL
Political cynicism
Political ideology

Figure 7.1 A sequence for environmental problem solving. The progression can be deflected by negative assessments at the critical evaluation points (1–7). The shaded items represent targets for tackling if the progression is to proceed.

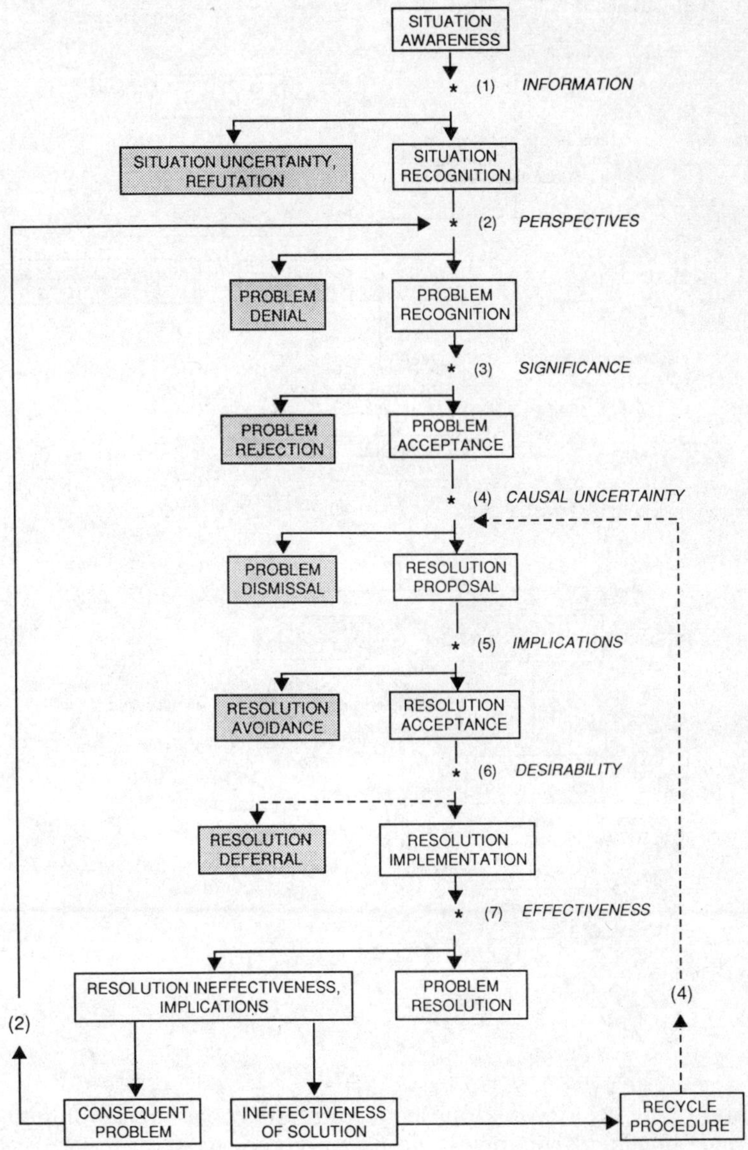

Figure 7.2a Role of the AKTESP barriers (from Figure 2.1) in the sequence shown in Figure 7.1. (a) From situation significance to resolution proposal. (b) From resolution proposal to problem resolution.

PROBLEM SPECIFICATION

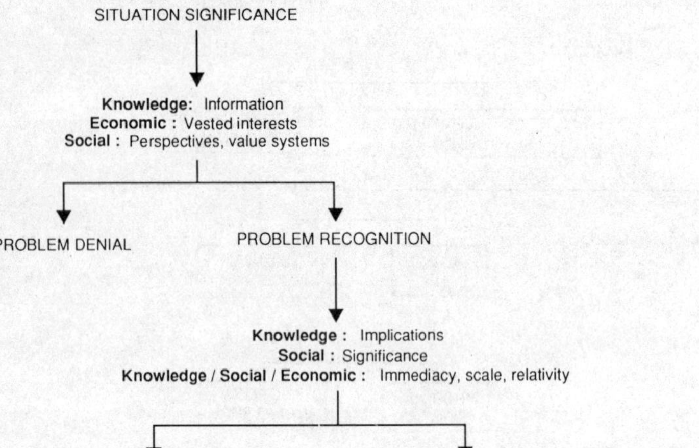

RESOLUTION FORMULATION

Knowledge: Inadequacy / casual uncertainty, rejection,
Technological : Inappropriatenesss, uncommunicated, unavailability, complacency
Economic : Vested interests
Social : Attitudes, Values

PROBLEM DISMISSAL

RESOLUTION PROPOSAL

Figure 7.2b From resolution proposal to problem resolution.

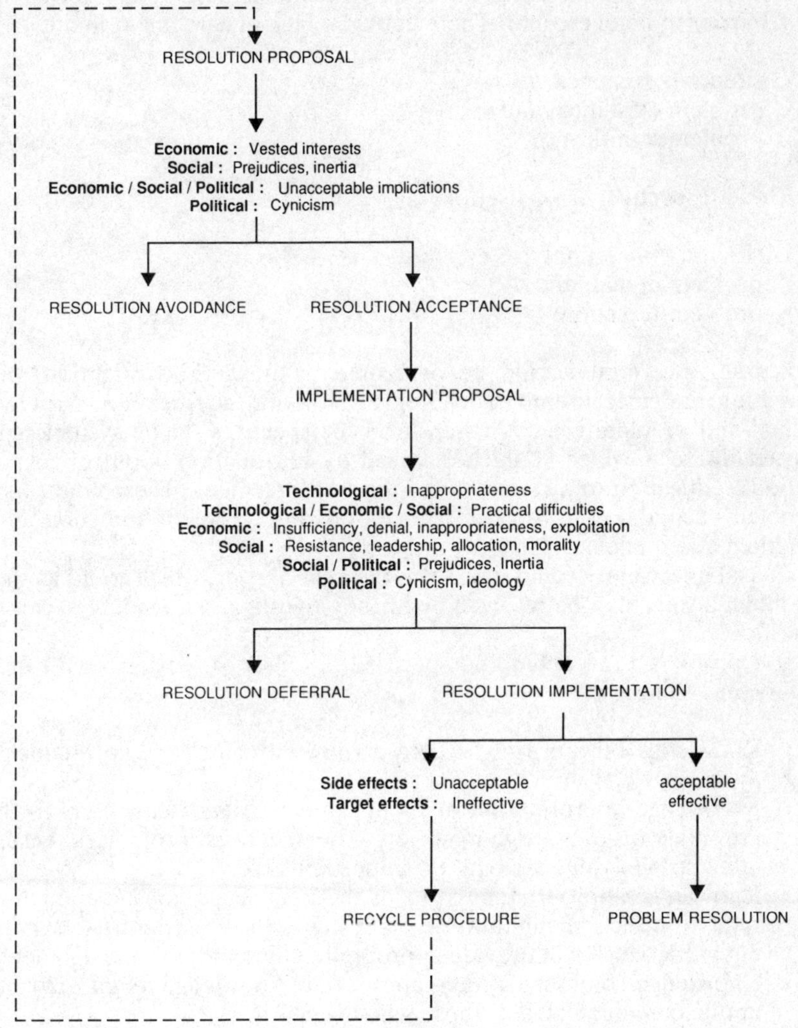

problem-solver is then to obtain situation recognition, problem recognition and acceptance and resolution proposal, acceptance, implementation and effectiveness.

The original AKTESP barriers identified in Figure 2.1 can now be nested in this sequence, as suggested in Figure 7.2. A lack of *agreement* forms the first barrier to be overcome. There could be lack of agreement about:

(1) situation existence;
(2) problem existence; and
(3) problem significance.

These respectively give rise to:

(1) situation uncertainty;
(2) problem denial; and
(3) problem rejection.

Situation uncertainty could be overcome by further investigation, observation and measurement, leading to situation clarification. Problem denial and problem rejection stem from perspectives, value systems and vested interests which could be tackled by information about effects of actions, education of awareness and legal enforcement. These could turn problem denial into problem recognition and problem rejection into problem acceptance.

Causal uncertainty could then form the next barrier, which could lead to problem dismissal or be resolved by further investigation, leading to causal clarification.

If a problem is accepted and specified, *knowledge* barriers could then intervene. Among these are:

(1) Knowledge existence – whether we know the causes and how to tackle them.
(2) Knowledge interpretation or significance barriers. This refers to the use made of knowledge in society – perspectives, prejudices, vested interests and value systems are important here.
(3) Knowledge appropriateness: (a) is the knowledge holistic enough to refer to effects thoughout the ecosystem? (b) are scientists carrying out work which will provide appropriate guidelines for management?
(4) Knowledge communication – appropriate knowledge might exist but not be communicated to those who needed it.

These could be tackled by:

(1) further scientific research;
(2) information and education;

(3) education of scientists;
(4) improved communication of appropriate and relevant knowledge.

If knowledge existed, is seen as significant and appropriate and is communicated to those who needed it, the next barriers are seen as *technological*. Such barriers are of three types:

(1) Technological answers may not exist.
(2) On the other hand, complacency may exist because of the feeling that we do have technological answers to all our problems.
(3) The technology may also be inappropriate, in terms of:
 (a) promoting environmental well-being and self sustainability; or
 (b) appropriateness for a society in question.

These can be tackled by:

(1) encouragement and financial support for technological innovation;
(2) education of awareness;
(3) learning from past experiences, awareness of technological appropriateness and awareness of the social contexts involved.

If appropriate technology exists and can be used effectively, the barriers become ones involving *economic, social* and *political* factors which could lead to *resolution avoidance* and/or *resolution deferral*. Economic barriers involve:

(1) a lack of perceived cash benefit;
(2) a lack of acceptance of causal responsibility and its financial implications;
(3) a situation where short-term economic accounting was involved; and
(4) an exploitative economic order.

These could be tackled by:

(1) stressing long-term benefits and stressing the value of non-cash benefits, either in cash terms or terms of life quality;
(2) minimising causal uncertainty and educating for acceptance of responsibility;
(3) stressing the long-term economic benefits of conservation options; and
(4) the evolution of economic order by stressing that environmental and economic objectives are not merely compatible but convergent.

If economic barriers could be overcome, then *social* barriers could exist. These involve:

(1) the resistance to new ideas because of perceptions, beliefs and values;
(2) inadequate involvement of community leaders and a diffuseness of the decision-making structure;
(3) social organisation in terms of land tenure; and
(4) dilemmas over the morality of induced social change.

These could be tackled by:

(1) attitude education and the demonstration of benefits in an effective and relevant manner;
(2) identification and involvement of the key people in society;
(3) reforming land tenure so that people reap the benefits of their own efforts; and
(4) addressing peoples' own self-perceived needs.

Lastly, *political* barriers might exist if no

(1) practical or
(2) ideological advantages could be seen in problem-solving.

Overcoming these situations involves:

(1) stressing electoral advantage, through voting popularity, or
(2) stressing ideological advantage by reinforcing and demonstrating the value system of a political institution.

This involves neither adopting an unrealistic, blind, green fundamentalism nor a cycnical stance that nothing can ever be made greener because of human greed or exploitation. Rather, it involves bringing green policies into existing regimes and thereby allowing the regimes to evolve in a greener direction. This means being realistic about human limitations while simultaneously not letting go of the ideal of striving for the ultimate goal of the wide adoption of green policies – a pragmatic idealism.

The Utility of Barrier Analysis: Case Studies of Environmental Problems

This analysis might seem logical according to what we have suggested as important so far. But how well does it stand up when applied to specific environmental problems? Can we identify specific barriers in all cases, and is such an identification helpful? The only way to attempt to answer these questions is to discuss the barriers in the contexts of such specific issues.

In this context, it should be stressed that this book was written in 1989 and that events can move very quickly. What could be an appropriate evaluation of the state of a problem one year might be irrelevant the next. For example, an analysis of the destruction of the ozone layer carried out

Figure 7.3 Template for mapping out the progression of specific environmental problems. On the right-hand side, the sequence finds no barriers and proceeds to resolution. The shaded items on the left represent barriers which have to be overcome by the items shown in the centre. Subsequent diagrams show how the progression of specific problems can be drawn as pathways of progress of inaction, thus highlighting the inaction barriers as targets for action.

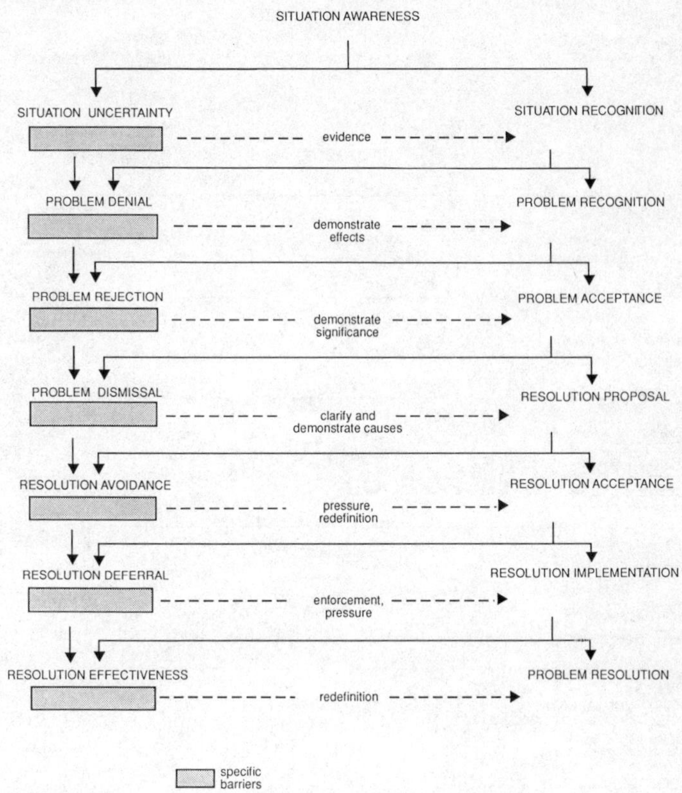

in 1988 might have concluded that the most important barrier to problem solution was a technological one – that aerosol manufacturers should find some propellant other than CFCs. We would also have encountered disputes as to whether CFCs were involved at all – causal uncertainty – and problem denial from those with vested interests. These barriers have since been substantially overcome, with technological innovation rapidly following, so that only a small proportion of CFCs now come from propellants. Today the problems are more of an economic and political nature, in that it is important to attempt to persuade all countries to implement effective measures and not to indulge in problem rejection.

In this analysis, we shall work in turn through each barrier so far identified and as summarised in Table 7.1 and Figures 7.1. and 7.2. Thus

Figure 7.4 Pathway of the ozone-hole problem. Resolution avoidance, deferral and ineffectiveness are highlighted as targets for action.

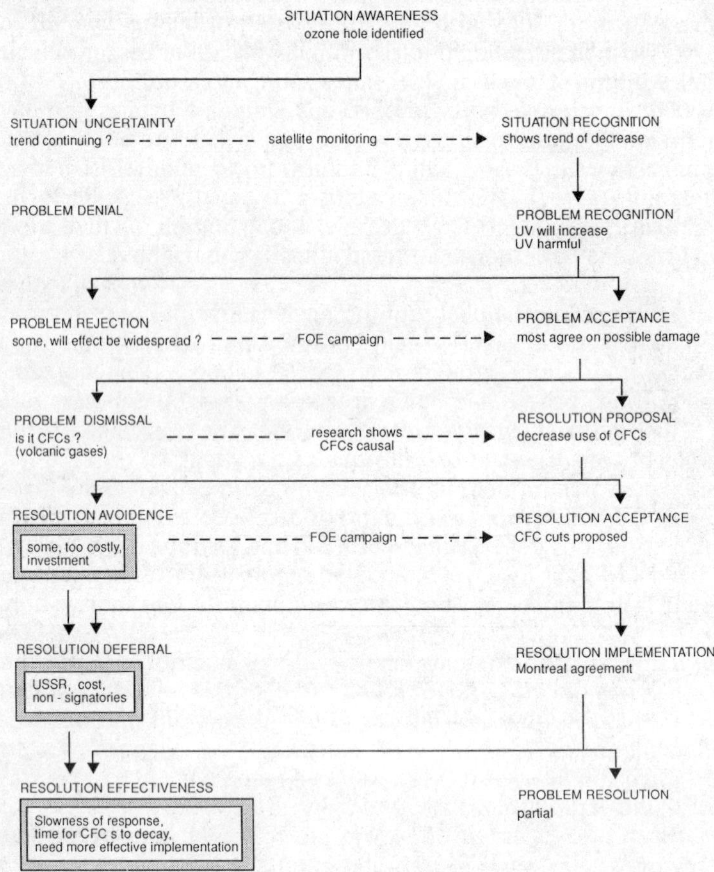

we shall first attempt to identify any agreement barriers. Then we shall assess whether adequate, appropriate knowledge exists and then move on to appropriate technology availability and the economic, social and political contexts. Finally, we shall assess whether the barriers are fundamental ones of attitude or whether they are involved with practicalities, which we can call facilitation barriers.

In each case, we shall use a template diagram, as shown in Figure 7.3. and then specify the relevant steps and barriers appropriate to each case and also indicate how the barriers have been or might be overcome. It should be reiterated that subsequent events may have rendered some of the assessments out of date, but the intention is to assess the utility of the

Figure 7.5 Pathway of the ozone-pollution problem. Problem dismissal is evident as a target for action on research to specify effects.

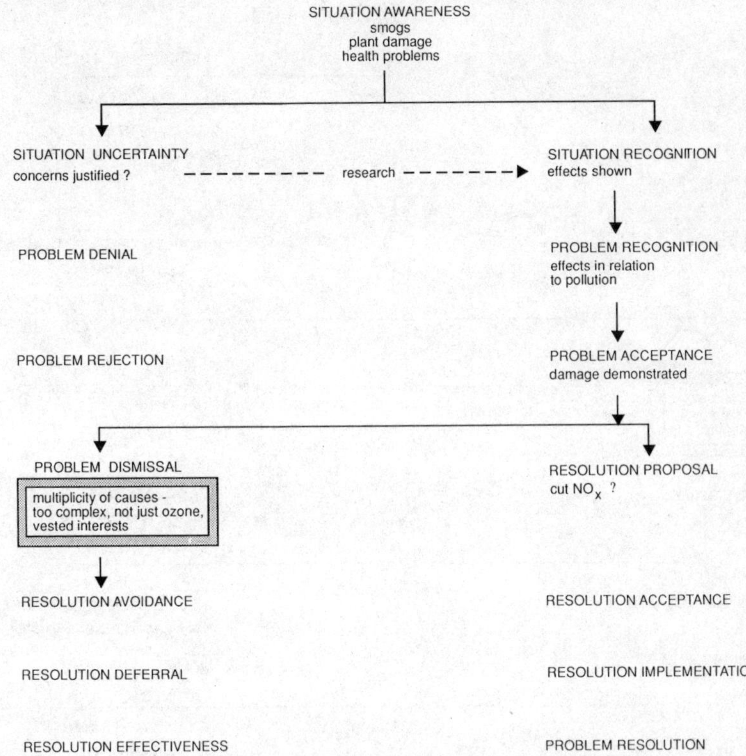

approach, rather than to provide an up-to-the-minute assessment of the problem.

We first consider the problem of ozone depletion (Figure 7.4). Once there was a situation awareness, the situation was confirmed and recognised. Some problem rejection and dismissal existed but was countered by campaigns and research – that is, the causal uncertainty was tackled by scientists. This led to problem acceptance and resolution proposal. Resolution avoidence also existed in relation to vested interests, but this was tackled by campaigns for problem awareness and also by the technological availability of alternatives. The barriers are now ones of resolution deferral and resolution effectiveness, especially in relation to the time needed for improvements to appear, and the political one of a lack of acceptance by all countries.

An *ozone pollution* problem has been recognised (Figure 7.5), but causal uncertainty has led to problem dismissal. Vested interests have impeded technological developments.

This problem of lead in drinking water (Figure 7.6) has met with

Figure 7.6 Pathway of the problem of lead in drinking water.

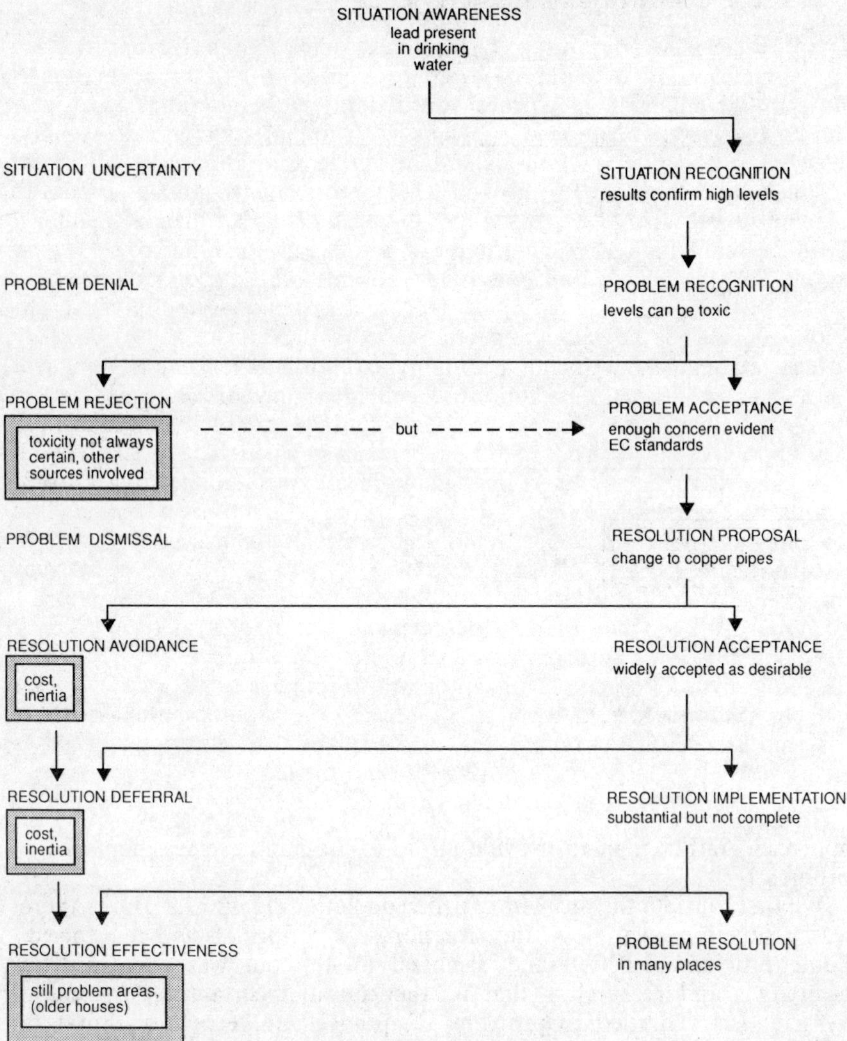

widespread recognition and acceptance, despite claims in some quarters that levels are not always high enough to give cause for concern or that the problem of toxicity is not always due to lead. Spurred on by the obligation to conform to EC standards, proposals made to solve the problem have received wide acceptance and implementation, although there has been some resolution avoidance and deferral, justified by economic and other political considerations.

Once it was established that there was a relationship between swan deaths and anglers' use of lead shot (Figure 7.7), rapid problem recognition

Figure 7.7 Pathway of the problem of lead angling weights.

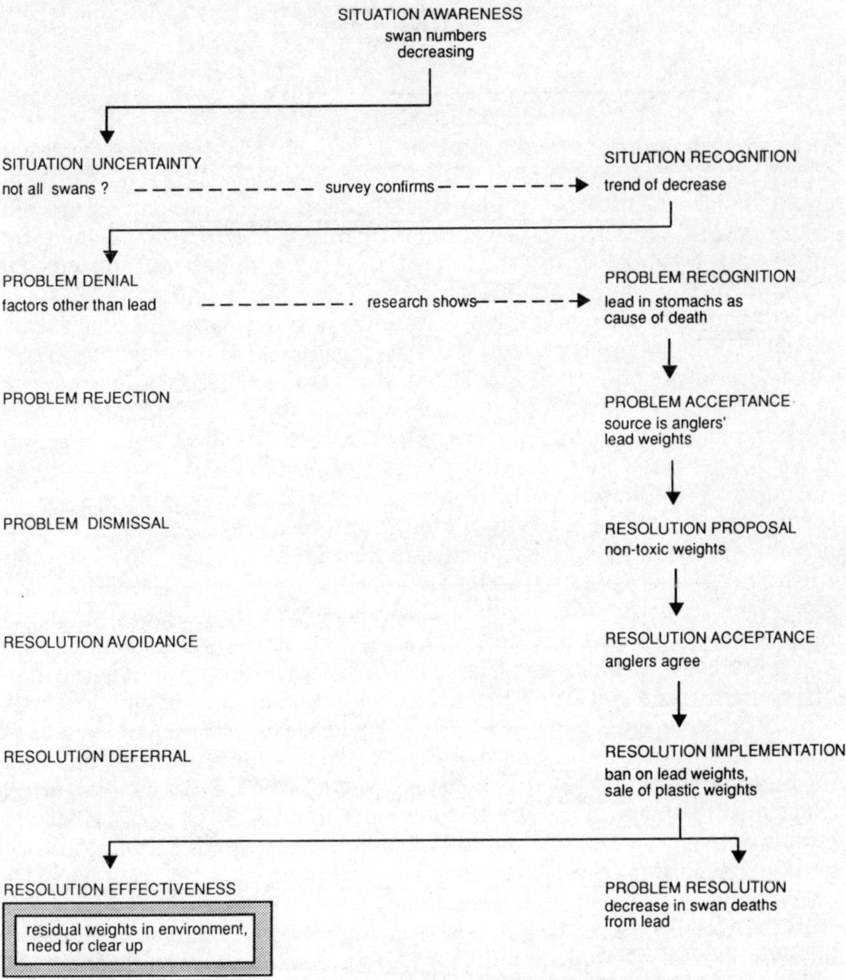

and acceptance ensued, followed by resolution, acceptance and implementation. This implementation has been successful, but the presence of residual lead shot in rivers and lakes should not overlooked.

Research was needed to show that lead was also widespread in the land environment. Attention was focused on the lead content in petrol (Figure 7.8), which gave rise to problem denial in some quarters because petrol is not the sole cause of the problem. Despite this, the problem was recognised and accepted because of the effects of toxicity, especially in children. The introduction of unleaded petrol received wide acceptance, although the cost of conversion of motor vehicles to run on unleaded has led to limited

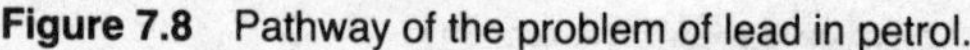

Figure 7.8 Pathway of the problem of lead in petrol.

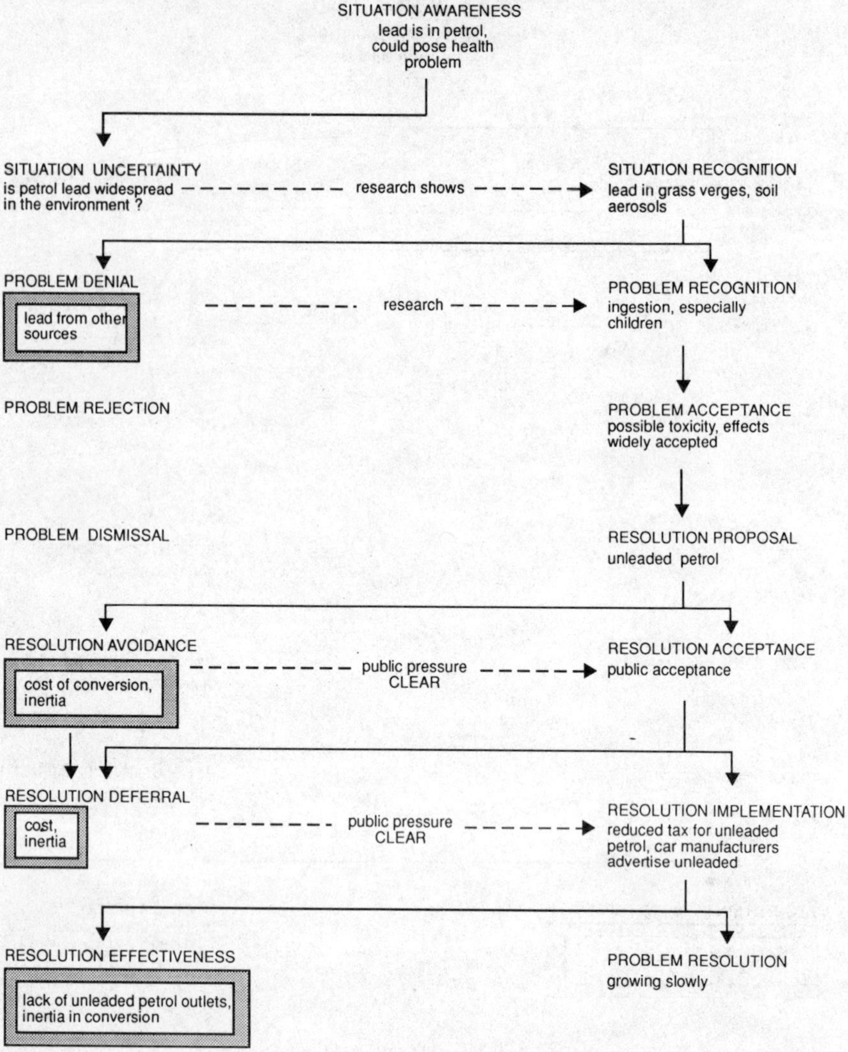

resolution avoidance and deferral. And even if the motorist is prepared to convert, unleaded petrol is still not as widely available as it could be.

There are many barriers to the solution of the problem of nitrates (Figure 7.9), but some resolution implementation has taken place. Barriers include arguments over sites of damge, the causal links, who is to pay (fundamental or limited solutions?) and relationships with wider agricultural and water-supply policies. Causal uncertainty, problem denial and rejection and resolution avoidance and deferral and political inertia are all major factors.

Figure 7.9 Pathway of the problem of nitrate in water.

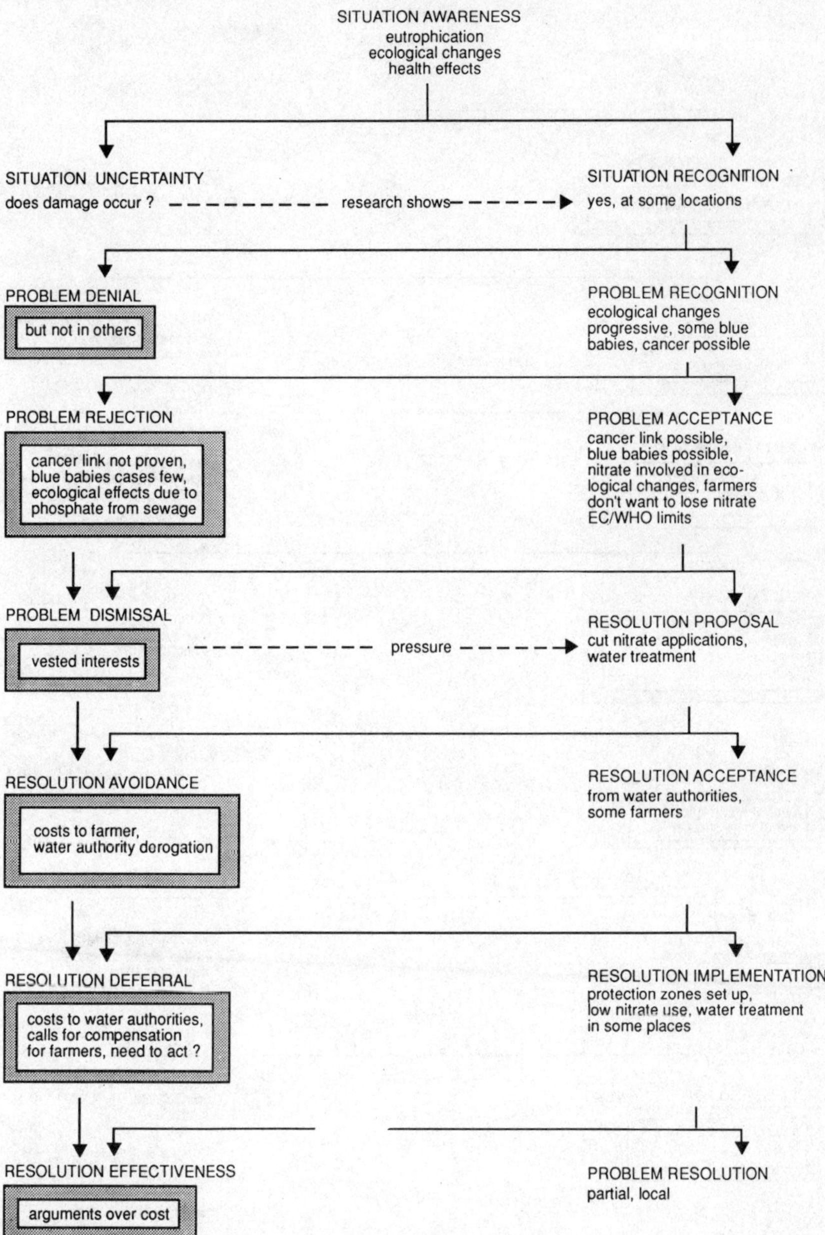

Figure 7.10 Pathway of the acid rain problem.

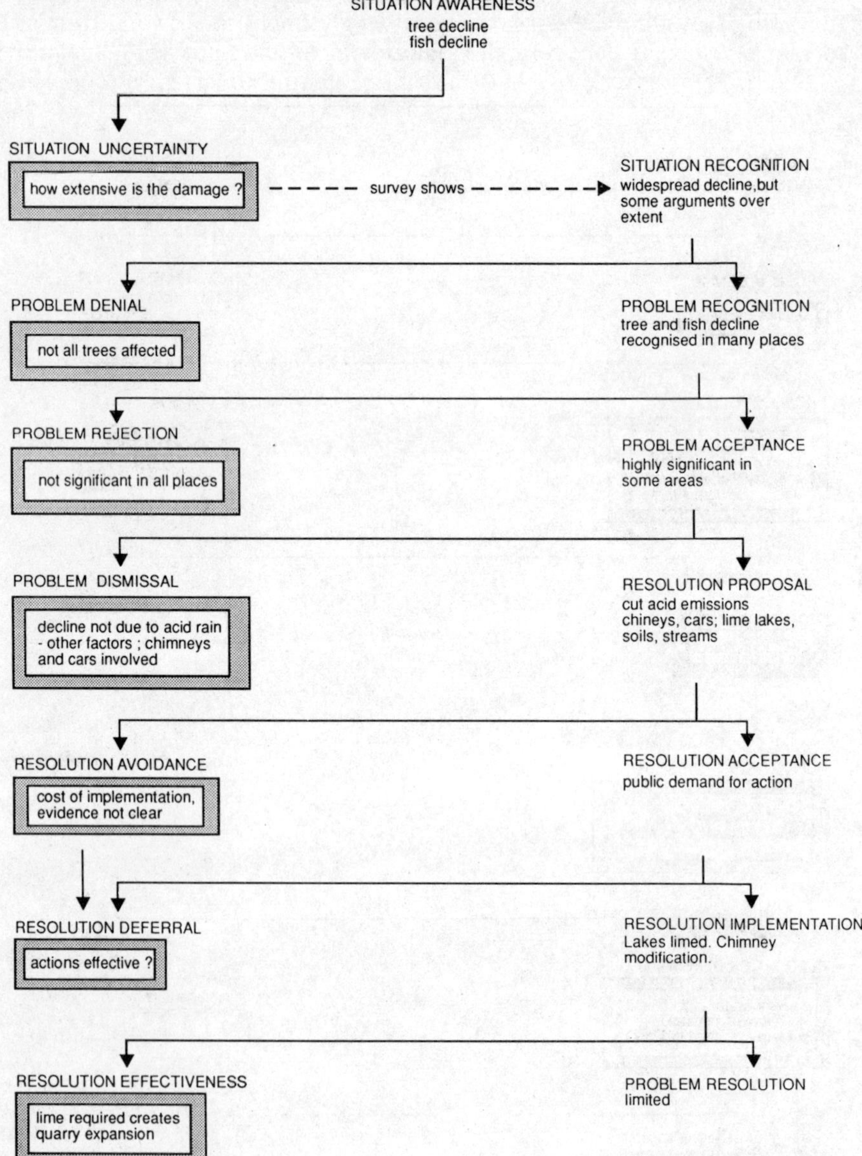

Figure 7.11 Pathway of the soil-erosion problem.

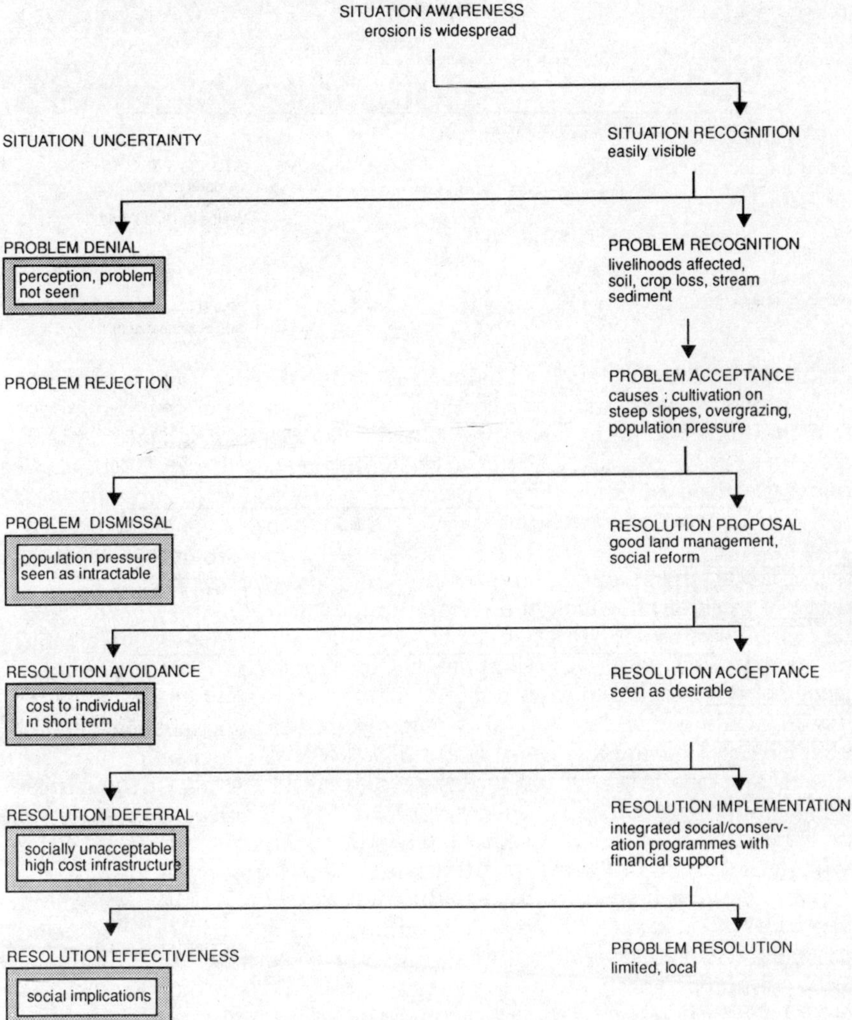

All the possible barriers are present in the acid-rain problem (Figure 7.10), especially causal uncertainty and political inertia.

There are few causal uncertainties as far as the problem of soil erosion (Figure 7.11) is concerned, but many perceptual, economic, social and political barriers present.

Despite much acceptance of the problem of pesticides (Figure 7.12), vested interests and economic factors have inhibited problem resolution.

It is apparent that causal uncertainty, vested interests and inertia are common, together with their underlying assumptions about lack of

Figure 7.12 Pathway of the pesticide probelm.

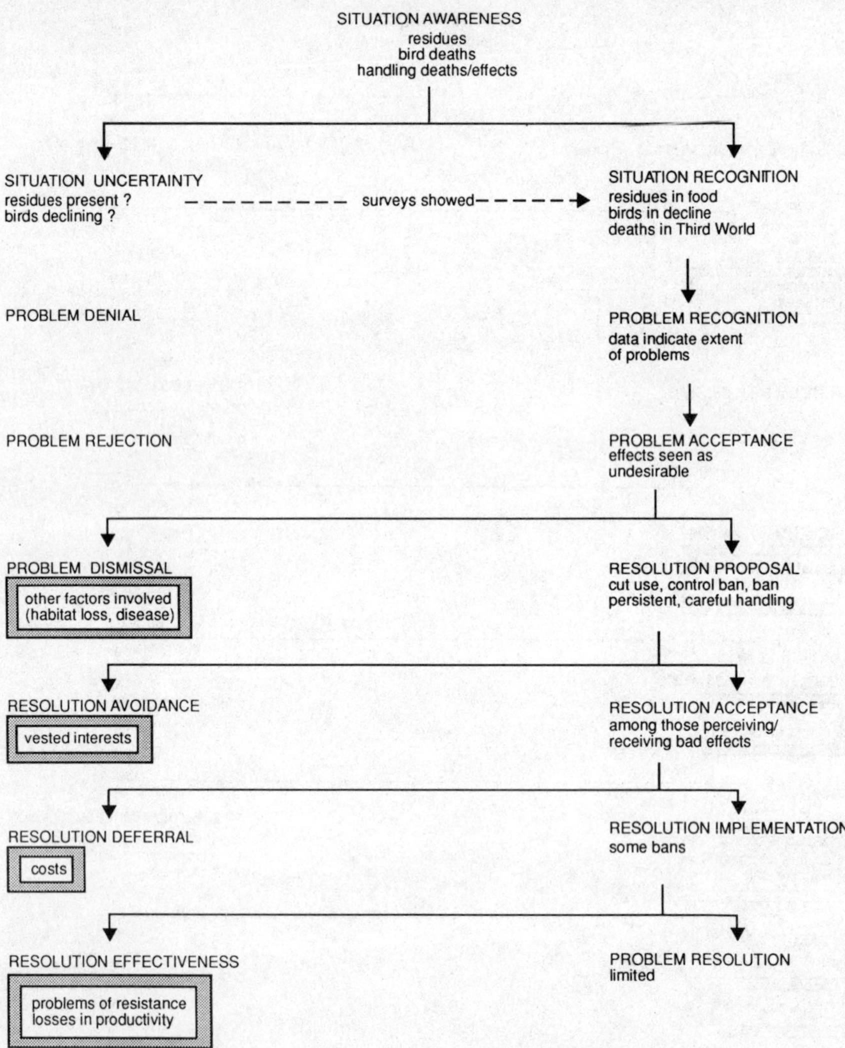

awareness in the scientific and political communities. This leads to problem dismissal, resolution avoidance and resolution deferral being commoner than situation uncertainty, problem denial and problem rejection. This places stress on the need for scientific research and for closer examination of political factors as well as the examination of underlying awareness, attitudes and values.

With reference to the AKTESP barriers (Chapter 2), both knowledge and economic, social and political barriers operate in problem-acceptance barriers while economic, social, political and technological barriers become dominant in resolution acceptance and implementation. Fundamental value and attitude barriers are present throughout and facilitation barriers are common in problem implementation.

It would seem that the environmental problems studied can be fitted into such an analysis. Moreover, while some experts may well not agree with particular analyses, it is a useful approach because it helps clarify the barriers and focus our attention on the specific barriers and thus also how we might tackle them.

We can be more specific than merely blaming 'the government' or 'the farmer', identifying specific instances of denial, rejection and dismissal of a problem, so that it becomes apparent whether the barrier is one of the problem not being recognised, or being recognised but not accepted as significant or being accepted but dismissed because of causal uncertainty and difficulties of target definition. If causal uncertainty exists, this may be due to knowledge inadequacy, rejection or inappropriateness or to knowledge communication barriers and we can act accordingly by promoting more relevant research and/or its communication.

If a problem is accepted and specified and a resolution is proposed, then we can identify whether the resolution is being avoided or accepted but deferred because of technological, economic, social or political factors, and if so, what they might be – technological inappropriateness, unavailability or complacency; economic insufficiency, denial of responsibility, inappropriateness or exploitation barriers; social barriers of resistance, leadership, allocation or social morality and factors of political cynicism or ideology. The analysis thus indicates how we can act specifically. We can then deal with barriers accordingly by promoting more appropriate developments, evaluations, attitudes, awarenesses and enforcements.

While we might suggest that a multitude of barriers might operate, they often condense into ones concerning awareness, knowledge or politics. Thus, there may be insufficient *awareness* and willingness to tackle the problem, or we do not *know enough* about the problem to be certain of the targets, or if we do know enough and are aware, then the stumbling block is one of politics. Awareness clearly relates to both corporate education policies and individual attitudes. Knowledge inadequacy refers to a lack of identification of causes and effects in the contexts of specific problems. This is a conceptual problem as much as it is a practical one. Political factors obviously relate to the problems people feel they care about and to legislation.

These can be tackled fundamentally by education of values and attitudes as well as by lobbying and argument at a more immediate level. Thus it is important to stress the economic and pragmatic benefits of a green policy and to promote a caring attitude to the earth. The first stresses self-interest, and the second is idealistic. These two are not, in the long term, in conflict but are two sides of the main endeavour of tackling environmental problems.

Overcoming the Barriers

Solutions to Specific Problems

Having identified the barriers to tackling specific problems, it would be useful to attempt to identify any needs which must be met in order to arrive at effective solutions. This will help us in evolving an agenda for action to overcome barriers.

If we are to solve the problem of *ozone depletion*, we need an effective global ban on CFCs. This must be backed up by research on other causes of ozone depletion and targeting actions. In addition, more research on upper atmospheric chemistry and its interrelationships, long-term modelling and monitoring should be carried out. This implies a need for international political intervention on CFCs and political investment in relevant research. In the meantime, a campaign of public education should be launched, aimed at eradicating the use of CFC-based products.

To counter the problem of *ozone pollution*, further research is needed on complex atmospheric processes, and their implications for human health and vegetation. Greater technological development of less-polluting car engines must be encouraged and ways must be found of using fewer cars. This implies a need for political investment in research into environmental processes, and technological development and viability of transport alternatives. Meanwhile, awareness of the effects of ozone pollution must be raised, and the alternative attitudes to transport encouraged.

Further research must be carried out into the effects of *lead pollution* on the environment, its health consequences and the specification and quantification of sources; the rate of conversion of lead-free water pipes and the availability of unleaded fuel should be increased. This implies the need for more money for research and more intervention on implementation. Meanwhile, a campaign of education is needed to reinforce public demand and market forces.

More research should be carried out on synergistic effects of phosphate and nitrate, and on the integration of water-resource needs with agricultural viability and crop-production levels. – an integrated strategy evaluation needs to be done. Money obviously needs to be made available for research and compensation.

More reliable surveys are needed of the damage caused by *acid rain*. Sources and transfer processes need to be identified more clearly. Careful consideration must given to evidence and consequences, before any intervention is made to implement a solution. Again, money must be made available for research and strategy evaluation, including energy needs and the desirability of alternatives.

If the problem of *soil erosion* is to be tackled, farmers need to be made more aware of the problem and shown the benefits of soil conservation. The related problem of population pressure needs to be tackled, and improvements to infrastructure must be made. These measures imply the

Figure 7.13 Summary of steps seen in Figures 7.4–7.12 which are necessary to progress from barriers (left) to problem resolution (right).

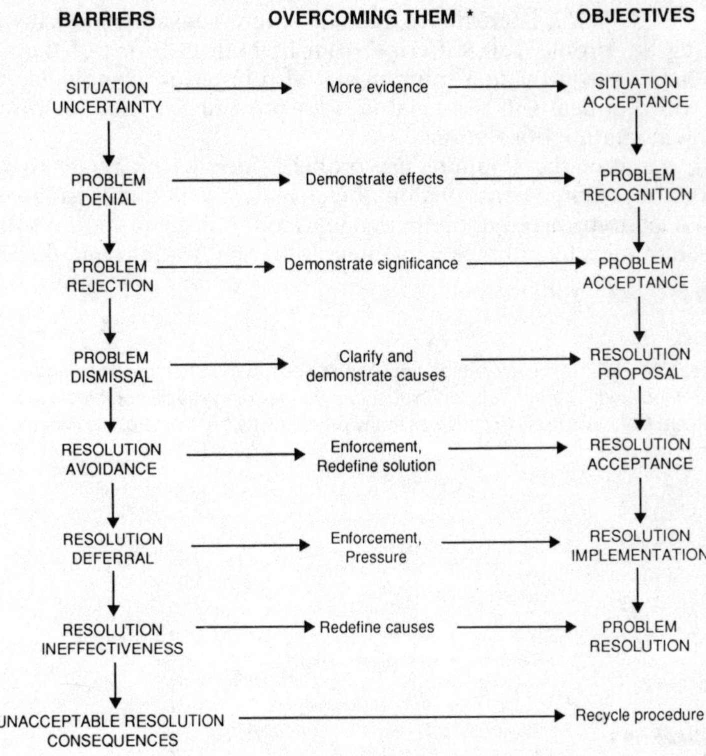

* Addressing attitudes and increasing awareness by education, demonstration, communication, argument, persuasion and discussion is implicit in overcoming most barriers.

need for money to be spent on education and on subsidies, as well as for co-operation among the various relevant agencies – concerned with social welfare, health and birth control – to ensure an integrated approach.

Finally, if the amount of *pesticides* finding their way into food and water supplies is to be cut, research must be carried out into effective alternatives, and in many cases lower productivity must be accepted. Money will have to be spent on the evaluation of strategies and on research, as well as on education. In addition, effective enforcement regulations, need to be drawn up.

It is clear that solution actions vary in specific cases, but there are some general features (Figure 7.13). First, money is needed for research into causes, processes and strategies; this is essential for effective solutions to be devised in terms of problem specification and target definition and in terms of the economic implications and social acceptability of solution strategies.

Second, education is crucial, especially where consumers are involved in causing the problem or suffering from it, both in terms of their own actions helping to provide a solution and also in terms of influence upon polical will. Political will is crucial in both providing money for research and implementation of solutions.

Third, many of the solutions are problem-specific but relate to wider issues and, if resource-conservation objectives are to be met – as discussed above – need to be acted upon in an integrated, holistic fashion if solution implementation is to embrace implementation ramifications and there is to be wide solution scope.

Figure 7.14 Web of relationships between major groups of environmental and human problems. The interrelationships mean that tackling specific problems in a piecemeal fashion is likely to cause as many problems as it solves; holistic thinking is necessary.

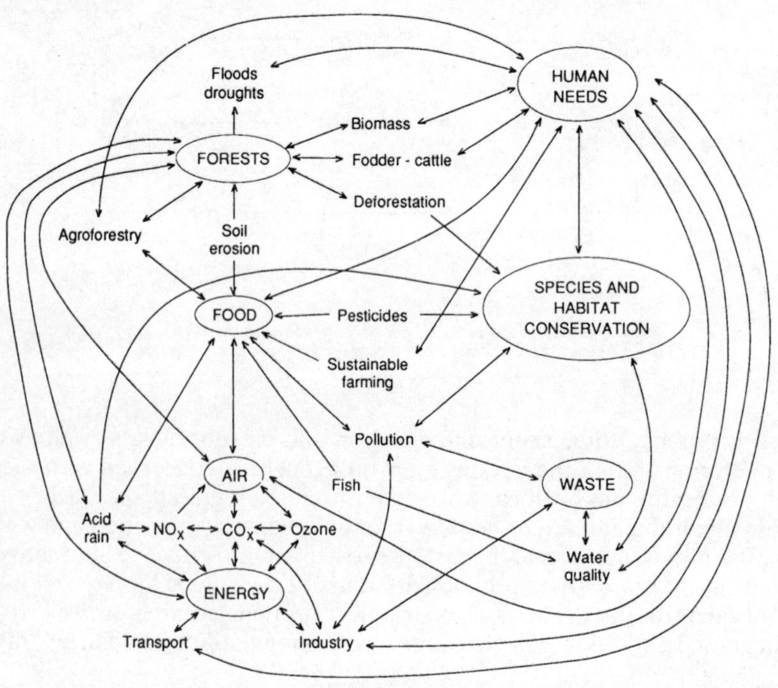

Integrated Solutions in a Holistic Framework

While the above focused on examples of specific issues, many of the solutions have indicated both the interrelatedness of specific problems and their wider ramifications through the economy and society as a whole. In these contexts, it is possible to group specific problems and to consider the possibility and desirability of integrated solutions. The groups considered are forests, food, air, waste, energy, human needs and species and habitat conservation. The interrelatedness of specific environmental problems is suggested in Figure 7.14.

Group 1: Forests. This group includes the need for biomass for such things as fuel, fodder and shelter. It also includes habitat for wildlife, and relates to floods, droughts and soil erosion in that a forest cover tends to mitigate the worst effects of these problems and their impact upon human survival.

Group 2: Food. This group includes the problems of feeding an expanding world population and includes the topics of sustainable agriculture which does not damage soil resources and the general topic of agriculture and environment, including the use of pesticides and habitat damage. Food from fresh water and the seas is also important.

Group 3: Air. This covers ozone, carbon dioxide and the greenhouse effect, acid rain and climatic change.

Group 4: Waste. This includes pollution of the water, air and land, as well as waste disposal.

Group 5: Energy. Under this heading we include renewable and non-renewable resources, recycling, transport, mining, and nuclear power.

Group 6: Human needs. This wide category includes the quality of life, income, security, resources, possessions, food, shelter, biomass, water, recreation, a pleasant environment, recreation, stimulation, social fabric, peace and stability, health, and population regulation in relation to resources.

Group 7: Species and habitat conservation. This covers extinction, intrinsic value of wildlife, economy through tourism, emotional needs of people, product development from the wild.

This is by no means the only way to group problems – it is used here only as a basis for discussion. Each group of problems has a number of solutions in common. These group solutions and their implications are as follows:

Group 1: Plant more trees, but as social forestry as well as commercial timber. This will relieve pressure on nautural forest, minimise erosion, droughts and floods, help air quality, provide energy, and meet human needs.

Group 2: Grow more food in a sustainable fashion, minimise soil loss. This will meet human needs in relation to numbers of people.

Group 3: Improve air quality. This will contribute towards human needs and improve habitat conservation.

Group 4: Reduce pollution of water, air and land resources. This will likewise contribute towards and improve habitat conservation.

Group 5: Increase dependence on renewable energy. This will conserve the environment, meet human needs, cause less waste and help habitat conservation.

Group 6: Increase human security through resource conservation. This will reduce conflict over resources and the need for exploitation.

Group 7: Increase conservation, not just in nature reserves but also on all land. This will meet human needs.

What emerges from this is that fundamental, integrated solutions are better than piecemeal solutions to specific problems and that taking the steps of social forestry, agroforestry, sustainable agriculture, birth control, reducing pollution, using renewable energy sources and improving conservation gives greater human security and the stimulation of a pleasant environment.

It would be naive to be hopelessly utopian about this; however, at least our solutions are clarified. It is clear that there are no environmental problems, only human ones. The biggest challenge is to carry out our cost accounting not just in financial terms, but in terms of the quality of life, sustainability of resources and stewardship of wildlife and habitats.

Several attempts have been made to tackle environmental economics in some of these terms, as mentioned in Chapter 6. Odum, for example, of the Institute of Ecology at Athens, Georgia, USA, has promoted the costing of habitats and wildland resources in terms of both real estate equivalents and of equivalent costs of processes and resources. His team (Gosselink, *et al.*, 1974; Odum, 1976), studied wetlands, costing out the value of fisheries, food production and waste removal, coming up with dollar figures for total life-support value. More general approaches are found in Cottrell (1978), Robinson (1986) and Baumol and Oates (1988), while Pearce *et al.* (1989) provide a more comprehensive analysis. Of key importance are the distributions of the costs and of the benefits of environmental programmes, and a key difficulty lies in sharing out international costs among nations. If the analysis of O'Riordan (1976) is correct (Figure 6.2) – that the benefits of an exploitative strategy are greater, in the short term, than those of a conservation strategy, where the benefits only show in the long term –

then the challenge lies in paying for conservation strategies in the short term until the long-term benefits can accrue. Idealists may argue that this could involve diversion of money from defence or other budgets, but this requires considerable political rethinking for many nations.

That long-term benefits could accrue is evidenced by the example that floods in India costs some 20 billion rupees every year, including the cost of bank construction for flood prevention (Agarwal *et al.*, 1987). Afforestation of the headwaters could mitigate this, reducing flood-damage costs while also providing biomass for local populations if enacted through social forestry (Trudgill, 1989). However, this would require holistic thinking on the part of forestry, water and agricultural planners.

We began this chapter by considering individual problems and what is needed to tackle them; we conclude by saying that they are interlinked both with each other and with the quality of human life. Thus, unless we can think and act holistically by dovetailing forestry, agriculture, water, soil, wildlife, industrial and economic policies in a forward-looking way that is both remedial and preventive, we shall continue to stagger from crisis to expedient solution and back to crisis. Policies and politicians should be able to gain kudos not just from specific problem or crisis solution but from far-sighted, forward-looking holistic thinking, making adjustments to suit economic, social and political circumstances, but never losing sight of holistic ideals.

Environmental Awareness

We have stressed the importance of environmental awareness in overcoming barriers to problem resolution. One of the spurs to resolution implementation is how much people care about environmental issues. What, then, do people care about? In this context, it is of interest to see the results of a European Community (EC, 1986) survey which included an assessment of the environmental issues people care about most. These were damage to sea life and beaches by oil tankers and the disposal of nuclear waste. Pollution of rivers and lakes also figured highly, but drinking-water purity evoked little concern. Also with low ratings of concern were landscape deterioration and air pollution. These concerns came below those about the deplction of forest resources, the extinction of animals and plants and possible climatic changes. Landscape deterioration and pollution tended only to be strong issues where local problems were perceived to be occurring (see Table 7.2).

When asked if they would be prepared to accept higher prices or lower economic growth to pay for environmental improvement, some 60 per cent of the 10,000 respondents showed their willingness to accept this by saying that priority should be given to environmental protection. Most concern was expressed about the environment in West Germany and the Netherlands, least in Ireland and Belgium.

These data suggest not only that is there an uneven perception of problems

Table 7.2 Public attitudes to the environment: responses to a survey of EC citizens.

Issue	% People who expressed a great deal of concern on the issues
Damage to sea life and beaches by oil tankers	45
Disposal of nuclear waste	45
Depletion of forest resources	36
Extinction of plants and animals	36
Pollution of lakes and rivers	35
Possible climatic change	30
Landscape deterioration	12
Air pollution	8
Drinking-water purity	6

and their significance, but also that there is still a long way to go in increasing environmental awareness. If so few people express great concern, and if we are right in stressing the importance of awareness, then this must represent a substantial barrier to be overcome.

Environmental Policies

At the other end of the scale from personal awareness, corporate, national and international policies are an important consideration in overcoming the barriers to environmental improvement. We often find a high degree of greenness in policies, even though implementations may fall short of ideals. To illustrate the potential of such policies in overcoming barriers, we can again use an EC example. European Year of the Environment activities related to the objectives of EC environmental policies which have been evolving since 1972. An early statement stressed the protection and improvement of the quality of the environment, the protection of human health, and the prudent and rational use of natural resources. Subsequent amendments involved the concepts of the prevention of pollution, the control of pollution at source, the integration of environmental protection requirements into other community policies and the 'polluter pays' principle. Also stressed later were the potential benefits and costs of actions or lack of actions. Of these, the aspect of integration into other aspects of community policy and the use of cost–benefit analysis have been seen to restrain EC actions. More recently, greater emphasis has been placed on policy integration (for example between agricultural and environmental policies) and on enforcement. The main principles of the EC environment policy approved by the Council of Ministers in 1973 are as follows:

1. Prevention is better than cure – the policy should prevent nuisances at source rather than merely counteract their subsequent effects.
2. The polluter must pay – thus the cost of preventing and eliminating nuisances must be borne by the polluter.
3. Action to control pollution should be taken at the appropriate level and the EC and its member states must actively co-operate in international initiatives dealing with the environment.
4. EC environment policy should aim, as far as possible, at the co-ordinated and harmonised development of national policies, without hampering progress at the national level.
5. Environmental policy can and must be compatible with economic and social development.
6. Care must be taken to ensure that activities in one state do not adversely affect the environment in other, and that major environmental policies in individual countries must no longer be planned and implemented in isolation.
7. The EC and its member states must take account of the developing countries in formulating their environmental policies.

The keynote theme is that the ultimate purpose of environmental poliy is to safeguard and improve the quality of life for the existing population and for future generations. The principle benefit of this is the limitation of environmental damage arising from previous neglect. While this may bring short-term costs to individuals, organisations and member states, there is hope for the future in that environmental improvements generally bring long-term economic benefits. Future generations will be able to judge from continued and extended monitoring programmes whether the resolutions and policies have been merely hopeful, worthy statements or the foundation for effective actions.

The fact that there is no lack of worthwhile policies at this level once again stresses the role of attitude education and political economy. Inadequacies of scientific evidence can be overcome if enough people in power and actively engaged in science are aware of the pressing needs for environmental evidence. In the short term, implementation of these policies is a matter of lobbying those in power; in the long term, attitude education is important so that there will no longer be a need for conflict between vested interests but a wide realisation that environmental and economic goals are not only compatible but mutually dependent.

An Agenda For Action

We have summarised the barriers discussed in detail in Chapters 2–6, and then seen how they might apply to specific problems. We have considered what specific solutions there might be to individual problems, and their

Table 7.3 Tackling the Barriers: An Agenda for Action

(a) EDUCATION (not only in schools and other educational institutions but also of the public, politicians and other decision-makers)

1. Awareness of the moral obligations and self-interest in tackling environmental problems, to promote motivation.
2. Awareness of effects of actions for tackling problem denial and rejection and promoting problem recognition and acceptance.
3. Awareness of relationships so that the significance of problems can be assessed for tackling problem dismissal.
4. Awareness of scientists of the need to provide knowledge that is appropriate to problem-solving.
5. Awareness of inadequacy of the 'technological fix' argument.
6. Awareness of the social contexts of technological innovation and thus of technological appropriateness.
7. Awareness of the moral need for accepting the finacial implications of causal responsibility.
8. Awareness of long-term economic benefits.
9. Awareness of those involved in promoting current economic orders of the need for self-sustainability and the integration of environmental and economic considerations.
10. Awareness of the importance of the enhancement of value systems.
11. Awareness of the importance of the self-perceived needs of a society and its individuals.
12. Awareness of political realities and the need for stressing political advantage in environmental problem solving.

(b) RESEARCH (involving both physical and social scientists)

1. Tackling situation uncertainty, promoting situation clarification.
2. Tackling causal uncertainty, promoting causal recognition and causal responsibility acceptance.
3. Problem specification, specifying causes, effects and mechanisms.
4. Maintenance of knowledge, but in a way that is appropriate and relevant to tackling specific problems as well as contributing to fundamental knowledge about how environments and ecosystems work and how people interact with them.
5. Development of appropriate technologies in terms of the self-perceived needs of societies, ease and costs of adoption, running costs, maintenance and replacement.
6. Environmental accounting: evaluation of cash and non-cash benefits, the latter both in cash terms and quality-of-life terms.
7. Identification of the key people in social structures and the specification of power structures and the decision-making process.
8. Evaluation of the self-perceived needs of societies and individuals.
9. Identification of land-tenure systems.
10. Evaluation of political systems and of political advantages of environmental problem-solving.

Table 7.3 Tackling the barriers: an agenda for action (continued)

(c) COMMUNICATION

1. Communication of appropriate knowledge to those involved in environmental management at every level, especially those regarded as laymen by scientists. This includes knowledge about:

   (a) situations;
   (b) problem specifications;
   (c) the means of tackling problems; and
   (d) the possible outcomes of various alternative management strategies.

2. Communication of the benefits which can accrue from environmental programmes in an effective, relevant and discursive way that is sensitive to people's self-perceived needs.

(d) LAW

1. Enforcement to deal with entrenched problem denial, rejection and dismissal.
2. Enforcement to deal with causal liability rejection.
3. To deal with land-tenure reform.

(e) FINANCIAL SUPPORT

1. Financial support for the funding of appropriate education, as in (a) above, both in education institutions and wider.
2. Financial support for the funding of appropriate fundamental and holistic environmental and socially relevant scientific research as in (b) above, and including the development of appropriate technology.
3. Financial support for the funding of effective and relevant communication in (c) above.

implications, and also stressed the importance of finding solutions in a holistic framework as well as the roles of awareness and policies. Taking all the barriers we have seen and the implications of their solution, we can now attempt to distil these into what might be an agenda for action. This is presented in Table 7.3, which lists what we should be trying to promote in order to overcome the barriers we have discussed in this book. It is divided into objectives for education, research, communication, law, and financial support.

What is striking about Table 7.3 is the large number of education objectives identified (using 'education' in both its formal sense of teaching and its wider sense of bringing information and awareness to all people). However, the fact that fewer objectives are identified in the areas of research, communication, law and finance in no way detracts from the importance of these. Nevertheless, if it is true that the most important set of objectives concerns education, this suggests that progress will take time, that it is not enough simply to pass a few laws or to throw money after the problems, and that the significant barriers constituted by our attitudes and level of awareness will take time to tackle.

The veracity of the conclusion about educational needs can probably be assessed by the fact that when discussing individual barriers in detail, we could identify perspectives, beliefs, value systems and vested interests as common factors in so many cases. This can be related to the notion that if people really want to tackle something, they will, and that if they do not, they will not. If people identify a research need, it quickly becomes a priority; if there is a communication barrier, it quickly breaks down in the face of demand; and if there is a perceived lack of money, it is soon forthcoming if the demand is strong enough. Thus, problem identification, awareness, demand and and response are closely related.

This also relates to the increasing responsiveness of industry and retail outlets to consumer pressure as a result of education and increased environmental awareness. For example, television advertisements now routinely proclaim that a product is 'ozone friendly' or 'environment friendly' and organically grown vegetables and phosphate-free detergents are now widely available in supermarkets. There is a clear market response and advantage in following and reinforcing consumer awareness. Similarly, many politicians now espouse green credentials in relation to public awareness. Politicians in democratic societies are necessarily followers of public opinion, so that the education of public opinion is a crucial factor, if environmental problems are to be tackled successfully.

There is also the point of view that sensible laws simply legitimise what is generally accepted in society, so that if appropriate environmental laws are lacking, such an acceptance must be lacking. Enforcement in itself is thus probably not the only answer but again the education of attitudes is what is lacking; laws are perhaps also an admission of the failure of education in that if people do not want to behave in what society sees as a sensible fashion of their own volition, they must be made to. On the other hand, nothing moves so fast as when people actually want it to. Thus, it must be that a lack of appropriate attitudes is the key barrier throughout the stages we have described.

So, if environmental problems continue, we can only conclude that we are generally lacking in motivation and awareness, despite the high profile of environmental education and green pressure groups in many of our societies, and time and effort are important in changing this situation – as indeed it is changing at the moment, with a far greater public awareness of environmental issues in the early 1990s than there was in the early 1980s. Thus, if it is seen as distressing that time for education is necessary for environmental ideas to work through, it should also be seen as comforting that the process is already in hand – where public awareness goes, consumer-orientated responses and political actions will surely follow.

If we therefore talk of fundamental barriers, involving attitudes and motivation, and of barriers to facilitation, the first set involves the will to do anything, the second involves overcoming barriers concerned with ways of doing something once the will has been established. Research, communication, law, financial support and political can then be seen as facilitation barriers which will be raised or lowered in accordance with how far we overcome the fundamental attitude barriers through education.

Conclusions

The whole purpose of this book has been to see how progress might be made in tackling environment problems by looking at what seems to have stopped us in the past. It then attempts to be prescriptive as to future needs. The barriers identified have been many (and indeed probably partial, coloured by individual experience and the availability of information) and more could probably have been identified. However, those which we have seen can now be used to highlight areas of future endeavour. These areas are grouped under the headings of science policy, education policy and politics – though while education policy has been separated out, it is nevertheless seen as fundamental to both science and politics.

Science Policy

Directed research

A clear need has emerged to identify the causes and sources of problems. While we have traditionally been engaged in what is often seen as fundamental science which could *then* be applied to problems, it is clear that we *also* need far more research which is *specifically directed* to addressing particular problems.

Fundamental research

This is not to say that we should neglect fundamental, pure science which is without any immediate practical application. This is because to do so may prejudice the needs of a future society when further unforeseen problems may arise and when we may then need to refer to our pool of fundamental knowledge to begin to tackle them. This is a lesson we can learn from the past. For example, at many pollution conferences in the past, there was often an ignorance expressed about conditions prior to the realisation of a problem; this could have been avoided by the prior monitoring of an environmental variable in what was then a seemingly unapplied context. We learn that research which seems unapplied at the time could have real value in the future. This also reinforced by the point of view which sees the intrinsic merits of pure research as part of the intellectual capital of a civilised society.

Applied research

There is a growing number of pressing needs in society concerning environmental problems to which we do not necessarily have adequate answers. While there are obvious difficulties in obtaining incontravertible proof in many cases, there should be more endeavour to minimise causal uncertainty. (For example, is flooding in Bangladesh due to deforestation or to Himalyan uplift? How far is acid rain due to power stations and how far to car exhausts?). This will minimise the 'innocent until proved' guilty stance of those standing to lose from the implementation of a solution and waiting for more evidence before they act. It can only improve government policy and action, which would be seen to be based on a more scientific footing rather than leave itself open to accusations of policy based on dogma, belief or ideology alone. It will also minimise the 'guilty until proved innocent' stance taken by many active environmentalists, calling for action when there is only limited evidence, and not enough of it firm evidence. Such an endeavour will help minimise the antagonism between vested interest groups which leaves the public caught up in a divisive debate and where confrontation rather than co-operation wastes otherwise useful energies.

Communication

A major challenge for scientists is also one of communicating the available information to the public and politicians in a comprehensible way. This is not easy because many situations are complex and multi-faceted. It involves specifying uncertainties clearly and placing clear probabilities upon causes and sources and on the likely outcome of actions.

Investment in research

To achieve this progress, a far greater investment in research programmes, equipment and manpower is needed. Environmental investigation is costly, especially in time if experiments and observations are to be replicated and observations specified more certainly. Investment in research institutions, equipment, staff and their training is crucial in this and is as urgent as any programme that could be thought of.

We need far more data on levels and concentrations of substances in the environment, far more tracing and tracking down to sources, far more research into the effectiveness of alternative control strategies and on the human health implications of environmental variables as well as more work on devising sustainable strategies and technologies.

There needs to be more research on the relationship between people's livelihoods, their political economy and the environment, especially that involving the economic implications of alternative environmentally desirable strategies and the environmental implications of alternative economic strategies.

In particular, a holistic environment management cost-accounting needs much greater attention. Viable political strategies can only be based on overall assessments and integration of economic viability and environmental desirability.

To achieve this we need far more people trained in environmental awareness – in a sound scientific fashion – and in environmental economic cost-accounting such as Pearce *et al.* (1989) have promoted. We also need more sociological inputs into technological developments (such as Blaikie, 1985, and Hallsworth, 1987, have promoted for soil erosion). We have to understand market forces and balance sheets as well as environmental processes, such as the hydrology and biology of pollution, if we are to pinpoint causes and tackle them in a fundamental but economically, socially and politically realistic way.

In particular, strategies for resolving traditional conflicts – between, say, employment and conservation, industry and pollution, and development growth and resource conservation – must be devised, but this again involves social and physical scientists working together and, ultimately, a need for people trained in both social and physical science.

Reference need only be made back to Figures 7.4–7.12. and to Tables 7.1–7.4 to see some of the research needs identified in both the physical and social sciences. Problem specification is a particularly crucial activity of social and physical science, as are the realisation of the ramifications of solution implementation and the derivation of holistic solution strategies. Science has a long way to go, but its progress depends not only on the willingness of its participants but more especially on the political will to make the investment of resources in developing science and scientists with a capability to tackle the breadth of the issues involved.

Education policy

Table 7.3 stresses educational needs, both formal and informal, both in schools and in the education of the public. Curriculum development and media presentations are crucial in the endeavour of raising environmental awareness.

Educational needs in the arena of science policy are also clear, especially in making problem specification, target definition, and solution implementation and scope into priorities which have both the involvement of people trained professionally and a public participating in them in an informed fashion.

Education is critical in goal definition. Without awareness of the consequences of actions (or inactions) goal clarification can only be partial and fall short of wider environmental goals. With greater involvement, there could be wider acceptance of goals and greater ownership of outcome among the public – instead of a materialistic alienation from both pragamatic politics and idealistic environmentalism.

Politics

Given a sound scientific basis – and a wide public awareness of it – it is less easy for politicians to escape from evidence and avoid implementing environmentally desirable policies and, conversely, easier for them to gain vote-catching credit for addressing themselves to these problems.

If problem specification and target definition are primarily scientific endeavours, goal definition, resolution implementation and scope of solution are primarily social and political concerns. In the long run, only society can decide where it wants to go and how to get there.

We have attempted to identify barriers which stop us tackling environmental problems. Our conclusions are that they involve aspects of volition, self-interest, altruism, goals, science, technology, education, economies, social structure, political will and public participation. It therefore seems that the crucial endeavour is not only for there to be debate between educationalists, scientists, environmentalists, politicians and the public about goals and implementation, but also for them to meet the substantial challenge of moving together in tackling the problems. This should be tackled not only in a way that is mutually beneficial to the conservation of the earth's resources, to the conservation of species and ecosystems and to human life, but also in a way that is also realistic about our current state and about our limitations.

Currently, there is still confrontation between those who appear to have higher ideals about a better earth – for people and for wildlife – and those who do not. The task of education, in its broadest sense, is to point out the common interests between economic viability, political stability and social well-being and a sustainable environment, rich in species and profitable and pleasant to live in. The task of science is to develop strategies for achieving this and to communicate them to the public. Armed with the appropriate education, the task of the public – and thus of politicians – is to evaluate the science, relate this to where they want to go, and then to try to get there.

Summary

In essence, this book has suggested that to solve environmental problems the necessary steps are to:

1. Decide on environmental goals.
2. Identify situations which fall short of these goals.
3. Specify the situations, the problems and their significance.
4. Propose resolutions.
5. Evaluate the relative merits of courses of action.
6. Identify the barriers which hinder goal formulation, situation and problem specification, problem acceptance, resolution formulation and resolution implementation.
7. Attempt to overcome the barriers and thereby to implement solutions.

References, Source Material and Further Reading

The text has not included a multiplicity of citations of references, sources of information or support for arguments which may have detracted from the essential themes of the book. However, the following pages not only provide references for those authors who are mentioned in the text, but also list the many sources I have drawn on as well as recommendations for further reading.

Chapter 3: Agreement Barriers

Agarwal, A., N. Kashyap, S. Narain, P. V. Ramana, U. Samarth, S. Sinha and M. Singh Kunwar, 1987. *The Wrath of Nature. The Impact of Environmental Destruction on Floods and Droughts*. Centre for Science and Environment, 807 Vishal Bhavan, 95 Nehru Place, New Delhi 110 019, India.

Agarwal, Anil and Sunita Narain, 1986. *The State of India's Environment, 1984–85. The Second Citizen's Report*. Centre for Science and Environment, New Delhi, India.

Blaut, J.M., R.P. Blaut, N. Harman and M. Moerman, 1959. A study of the cultural determinants of soil erosion and conservation in the Blue Mountains of Jamaica. *Social and Economic Studies*, **8**, 403–20.

Brown, L.R. and P. Shaw, 1982. *Six Steps to a Sustainable Society*. Worldwatch Paper no. 48.

Cape, J.N., I.S. Paterson, A.R. Wellburn, J. Wolfenden, H. Mehlhorn, P.H. Freer-Smith and S. Fink, 1988. *Early Diagnosis of Forest Decline*. Institute of Terrestrial Ecology, Natural Environment Research Council, Grange-over-Sands.

Carim, E.G. Barnard, G. Foley, D. de Silva, J. Tinker and R. Walgate (eds.) 1987. *Towards Sustainable Development*. The Panos Institute: Nordic Conference on Environment and Development, Saltsjöbaden, Stockholm, May.

Conway, G. (ed.) 1986. *The Assessment of Environmental Problems*. Imperial College, Centre for Environmental Technology, 48 Prince's Gardens, London SW7 2PE.

Department of the Environment, 1988. *Our Common Future: A Perspective by the United Kingdom on the Report of the World Commission on Environment and Development*. HMSO, London.

Elsworth, S., 1984. *Acid Rain*. Pluto Press, London and Sydney.

Fernie, J. and A.S. Pitkethly, 1985. *Resources, Environment and Policy*. Harper & Row, London.

Goldsmith, E. and N. Hildyard, 1986. *Green Britain or Industrial Wasteland*? Polity Press, Cambridge.

Harrison, P., 1987. *The Greening of Africa: Breaking Through in the Battle for Land and Food*. Paladin, London.

Hurd, L.E., M.V. Mellinger, L.L. Wolf and S.J. McNaughton, 1971. Stability and diversity at three trophic levels in terrestrial successional ecosystems. *Science*, **173**, 1134–6.

International Institute for Environment and Development (IIED) 1987. *Our Common Future. A Reader's Guide: The 'Brundtland Report' Explained*. IIED, Earthscan, 3 Endsleigh Street, London, WC1H 0DD.

International Union for Conservation of Nature and Natural Resources (IUCN) 1980. *World Conservation Strategy*, IUCN, Gland, Switzerland.

Macmillan, B., 1988. Lost and found. The case of the unknown cluster. *Geography Review*, **1**(3), 39–41.

MacArthur, R.H., 1955. Fluctuations of animal populations, and a measure of community stability. *Ecology*, **36**, 533–6.

Nicholson, I.A., I.S. Paterson and F.T. Last, 1980. *Methods for Studying Acid Precipatation in Forest Ecosystems*. Institute of Terrestrial Ecology, Natural Environment Research Council, Cambridge.

Park, C.C., 1987. *Acid Rain: Rhetoric and Reality*. Methuen, London.

Pepper, D., 1984. *The Roots of Modern Environmentalism*. Croom Helm, London.

Pickett, S.T.A. and P.S. White, 1985. *The Ecology of Natural Disturbance and Patch Dynamics*. Academic Press, London.

Porritt, J., 1984. *Seeing Green*. Blackwell, Oxford.

Rackham, O., 1986. *The History of the Countryside*. J.M. Dent, London

Redclift, M., 1984. *Development and the Environmental Crisis: Red or Green Alternatives*? Methuen, London.

Redclift, M., 1987. *Sustainable Development: Exploring the Contradictions*. Methuen, London.

Rose, C., 1988. *Acid Rain: It's Happening Here*. Greenpeace, UK.

Royal Commission on Environmental Pollution, 1983. *Lead in the Environment*, Cmmd. 8852. HMS0, London.

Shoard, M., 1980. *The Theft of the Countryside*. Temple Smith, London.

Trudgill, S.T., 1988. Environment today: A view of the future. *Geography Review*, **1** (4), 36–40. Ozone, **1** (29–34); Lead, **2** (38–40); The Nitrate **2** (5), 34–36.

van der Post, L., 1957. *Venture to the Interior*. Penguin, Harmondsworth.

van der Post, L., 1961. *The Heart of the Hunter*. Penguin, Harmondsworth.

van der Post, L., 1976. *A Far-off Place*. Penguin, Harmondsworth.

van der Post, L., 1976. *Story Like the Wind*. Penguin, Harmondsworth.

van der Post, L., 1986. *A Walk with a White Bushman*. Penguin, Harmondsworth.

Vohra, B.B., 1985. *Land and Water*. Indian National Trust for Art and Cultural Heritage; Environmental Series no. 2; 71 Lodi Estate, New Delhi 110 003, India.

Wijkman, A. and L. Timberlake, 1984. *Natural Disasters: Acts of God or Acts of Man*? Earthscan, London.

World Commission on Environment and Development, 1987. *Our Common Future* (the Brundtland Report). Oxford University Press, Oxford.

Chapter 4: Knowledge Barriers

Bull, D., 1982. *A Growing Problem: Pesticides and the Third World Poor*. Oxfam, Oxford.

Elsworth, S., 1984. *Acid Rain*. Pluto Press, London and Sydney.

Farman, J., 1987. What hope for the ozone layer now? *New Scientist*, **116** (1586), 50–4.

Haines-Young, R. and J. Petch, 1986. *Physical Geography: Its Nature and Methods*. Harper & Row, London.

Ko, M.K.W., J.M. Rodriguez and N.D. Sze, 1987. Antartic chemistry: Implications for global ozone changes. Abstract A11B-07 H, *EOS* (American Geophysical Union), **68**(16), 21 April, 271.

Meadows, D.H., D.L. Meadows, J. Randers and W.W. Behrens, 1972. *The Limits to Growth: A Report for the Club of Rome's Project on the Predicament of Mankind*. Earth Island Limited, London.

Milne, R., 1989. Leukaemia clusters may have genetic origin. *New Scientist*, 17 June, 39.

O'Sullivan, P.E., 1986. Environmental science and environmental philosphy. Part 1: Environmental science and environmentalism. *International Journal of Environmental Studies*, **28**, 97–107.

Park, C.C., 1987. *Acid Rain: Rhetoric and Reality*. Methuen, London.

Park, J.R. (ed.) 1988. *Environmental Management in Agriculture*. Belhaven Press, London.

Pereira, C., 1981. Future trends in watershed management and land development research. In R. Lal and E.W. Russell (eds), *Tropical Agricultural Hydrology: Watershed Management and Land Use*. Wiley, Chichester (see p. 466).

Platt, J.R., 1964. Strong inference. *Science*, **146** (3642), 347–53.

Steinbeck, J., 1960. *The Log from the Sea of Cortez*. Pan, London.

Tivy, J. and G. O'Hare, 1981. *Human Impact on the Ecosystem*. Olver & Boyd, Edinburgh.

Trudgill, S.T., 1988. *Soil and Vegetation Systems*. Oxford University Press, Oxford.

Tucker, A., 1985. Making scientific concerns clearer to the public, and public concerns clearer to the scientist. *The Guardian*, 9 May, 15.

Zelinsky, W., 1975. The demigod's dilemma. *Annals of the Association of American Geographers*, **65**(2), 123–43.

Chapter 5: Technological Barriers

Amphlett, M.B., 1989. *A Field Study to Assess the Benefits of Land Husbandry in Malawi*. Overseas Development Unit, Hydraulics Research, Wallingford, UK. OD/P 64.

Barrow, C., 1987. *Water Resources and Agricultural Development in the Tropics*. Longman Harlow. UK.

Boyden, J. and B. Pratt, 1985. *The Field Directors' Handbook: An Oxfam Manual for Development Workers*. Oxfam, Oxford.

Croxall, H.E. and L.P. Smith, 1984. *The Fight for Food: Factors Limiting Agricultural Production*. George Allen & Unwin, London.

Douglas, J.S. and R. A. de J. Hart, 1985. *Forest Farming*. Intermediate Technology Publications, London.

Harrison, P., 1983. *The Third World Tomorrow*. Penguin, London.
Harrison, P., 1987. *The Greening of Africa: Breaking Through in the Battle for Land and Food*. Paladin, London.
International Institute for Environment and Development/World Resources Institute, 1987. *World Resources 1987*. Basic Books, New York.
Pacey, A. and A. Cullis, 1984. *Rainwater Harvesting*. Intermediate Technology Press, London.
Rackham, O., 1986. *The History of the Countryside*. J.M. Dent, London.
Richards, P., 1985. *Indigenous Agricultural Revolution: Ecology and Food Production in West Africa*. Hutchinson, London.
Trudgill, S.T., 1988. Environment today: A view of the future. *Geography Review*, **1**(4), 36–40.
Twose, N., 1985. *Fighting the Famine*. Pluto Press, London and Sydney.
Walker, B., 1977. *Appropriate Technology: A Paper by OXFAM*, Council on International Development, Paper COID 77/21, Oxfam, Oxford.

Chapter 6: Economic, Social and Political Barriers

Agarwal, A., D. D'Monte and U. Samarth, 1987. *The Fight for Survival: People's Action for the Environment*. Centre for Science and Environment, New Delhi.
Amer, B., 1987. *Ethiopia, 1983–85: The Unecessary Tragedy*. Third World Publications, 151 Stratford Road, Birmingham B11 1RD.
Baumol, W.J. and W.E. Oates, 1988. *The Theory of Environmental Policy*. Cambridge University Press, Cambridge.
Beer, H. and Z. Rizvi (eds) 1986. *The Vanishing Forest: The Human Consequences of Deforestation*. Independent Commission on International Humanitarian Issues, Zed Books, London.
Blaikie, P., 1985. *The Political Economy of Soil Erosion in Developing Countries*. Longman, Harlow.
Blaut, J.M., R.P. Blaut, N. Harman and M. Moerman, 1959. A study of the cultural determinants of soil erosion and conservation in the Blue Mountains of Jamaica. *Social and Economic Studies*, **8**, 403–20.
Bowers, J.K., 1984. The subsidy element included in 'compensation' payments under the Wildlife and Countryside Acts 1981. Working paper, J.K.Bowers, School of Economic Studies, University, Leeds LS2 9TJ.
Braat, L.C. and W.F.J. van Lierop (eds) 1987. *Economic-Ecological Modelling*, Studies in Regional Science and Urban Economics, 16. Elsevier, Amsterdam.
Clarke, J., undated [1986?] *Ethiopia's Campaign against Famine*. Harney & Jones, 119–121 Falcon Road, London SW11 2PQ.
Committee for the Founding of the People's Democratic Republic of Ethiopia, 1987. *Ethiopia: From Feudal Autocracy to People's Democracy*. Addis Ababa.
Cottrell, A., 1978. *Environmental Economics*. Resource and Environmental Sciences Series, Edward Arnold, London.
Croxall, H.E. and L.P.Smith, 1984. *The Fight for Food: Factors Limiting Agricultural Production*. George Allen & Unwin, London.
Davis, R.M., G.S. Stacey, G.I. Nehman and F.K. Goodman, 1975. An approach to trading off economic and environmental values in industrial land-use planning. *Geographical Analysis*, **7**, 397–410.
Dogra, B., 1987. *Empty Stomachs and Packed Godowns: Aspects of the Food System in India*. Bharat Dogra, D-7 Raksha Kunj, Paschim Vihar, New Delhi 110063, India.

Freeman III, A. Myrick, 1982. *Air and Water Pollution Control: A Benefit–cost Assessment*. Wiley, New York.

George, S., 1988. *A Fate Worse Than Debt: A Radical New Analysis of the Third World Debt Crisis*. Penguin, London.

Goodland, R.J.A., 1988. Environmental implications of major projects in Third World development. Paper delivered to the Major Projects and the Environment conference, Royal Geographical Society, London, 14 November. R.J.A. Goodland, World Bank, Washington, DC 20433.

Gosselink, J.G., E.P. Odum and R.M. Pope, 1974. *The Value of a Tidal Marsh*. Center for Wetland Resources, Louisiana State University, Baton Rouge. LSU-SG-74-03.

Grainger, A., 1982. *Desertification: How People Make Deserts, How People Can Stop and Why They Don't*. Earthscan, IIED, London.

Harrison, P., 1983. *The Third World Tomorrow*. Penguin, London.

Harrison, P., 1987. *The Greening of Africa: Breaking Through in the battle for land and food.* Paladin, London.

Hudson, N., 1971. *Soil Conservation*, Batsford, London.

Hughes-Evans, D., 1977. *Environment Education: Key Issues for the Future*. Pergamon, Oxford.

Johnston, R.J., 1989. *Environmental Problems: Nature, Economy and State*, Belhaven Press, London.

Lowe, P., G. Cox, M. MacEwen, T. O'Riordan and M. Winter, 1986. *Countryside Conflicts: The Politics of Farming, Forestry and Conservation*. Temple Smith/ Gower, Aldershot.

MacIntrye, A.A., 1987. Why pesticides received extensive use in America: A political economy of agricultural pest management to 1970. *Natural Resources Journal*, **27**(3), 533–78.

Napier, T.L., 1989. The evolution of US Soil Conservation policy; from voluntary approach to coercion. Paper presented at the inaugural meeting of the World Association of Soil and Water Conservation Within the European Community, Coventry, England, January. T.L. Napier, Department of Agricultural Economics and Rural Sociology, Ohio State University, 2120 Fyffe Road, Columbus.

Odum, E.P., 1976. The coming merger of ecology and economics. Paper presented at Forging the Economic Quality of Life in Georgia seminar, Georgia Center for Continuing Education, Athens, GA. 26 March.

O'Riordan, T., 1976. *Environmentalism*. Pion, London.

Owens, S., 1986. Environmental politics in Britain: New paradigm or placebo? *Area* (Institute of British Geographers), 18 March, 195–201.

Pearce, D., A. Markandya and E.B. Barbier, 1989. *Blueprint for a Green Economy*. Earthscan, IIED, London.

Peberdy, M., 1985. *Tigray: Ethiopia's Untold Story*. Relief Society of Tigray UK Support Committee, YMCA Residential Centre, St Mary's Road, London W5 5RF.

Porritt, J., 1988. Geography and environmental education: An interview with Jonathon Porritt of Friends of the Earth. *Geography Review*, **2**(2), 24–6.

Price, B., 1986. Lead astray. In E. Goldsmith and N. Hildyard *Green Britain or Industrial Wasteland?* Polity Press, Cambridge.

Rahmato, Dessalegn, 1985. *Agrarian Reform in Ethiopia*. Red Sea Press, Trenton, NJ; Spokesman, Nottingham.

Ratcliffe, J., 1976. *Land Policy: An Exploration of the Nature of Land in Society*. Hutchinson, London.

Redclift, M., 1984. *Development and the Environmental Crisis: Red or Green Alternatives*? Methuen, London.
Redclift, M., 1987. *Sustainable Development: Exploring the Contradictions*. Methuen, London.
Robinson, S. (ed.) *Healthier Profits, Business, Success and the Green Factor*. The Environment Foundation, Ibex House, Minories, London, EC3N 1HJ.
Saberwal, S., 1986. *India: The Roots of Crisis*. Oxford University Press, Delhi.
Singh, R.B., 1987. *Planning for Rural Development*. Discovery Publishing House, Delhi.
Trudgill, S.T., 1988. (See Under Porritt).
Trudgill, S.T., 1989. Environment today: Forests for people. *Geography Review*, **2**(3), 29–32.
Turner, R.K. (ed.) 1988. *Sustainable Environment Management: Principles and Practice*. Belhaven Press, London.
Union of Socialist Geographers, London Group. 1983. *Society and Nature*. Terry Cannon, School of Humanities, Thames Polytechnic, Wellington Street, London SE18 6PF.
van der Post, L. 1976. *A Far-off Place*. Penguin, Harmondsworth.
Van Matre, S., 1979. *Sunship Earth: An Acclimatization Program for Outdoor Learning*. American Camping Association, Martinsville, IN.
Van Matre, S., 1974. *Acclimatizing: A Personal and Reflective Approach to a Natural Relationship*. American Camping Association, Martinsville, IN.
World Commission on Environment and Development, 1987. *Our Common Future* (the Brundtland Report). Oxford University Press, Oxford.

Chapter 7: Overcoming the Barriers

Agarwal, A., N.Kashyap, S. Narain, P.V. Ramana, V. Samarth, S. Sinha, and M. Singh Kunwar, 1987. *The Wrath of Nature. The Impact of Environmental Destruction on Floods and Droughts*. Centre for Science and Environment, 807 Vishal Bhavan, 95 Nehru Place, New Delhi 110 019, India.
Allaby, M., 1971. *The Eco-activists: Youth Fights for a Human Environment*. Charles Knight, London.
Alexandratos, N. (ed.) 1988. *World Agriculture Toward 2000*. Belhaven Press, London.
Arvill, R., 1967. *Man and Environment: Crisis and Strategy of Choice*. Penguin, London.
Baumol, W.J. and W.E. Oates, 1988. *The Theory of Environmental Policy*. Cambridge University Press, Cambridge.
Blaut, J.M., R.P. Blaut, N. Harman and M. Moerman, 1959. A study of the cultural determinants of soil erosion and conservation in the Blue Mountains of Jamaica. *Social and Economic Studies*, 8, 403–20.
Blaikie, P., 1985. *The Political Economy of Soil Erosion in Developing Countries*. Longman, Harlow.
Blum, A., 1988. Think globally, act locally, plan (also) centrally. *Journal of Environmental Education*, **19**(2), 3–8.
Bowonder, B., 1987. Environmental problems in developing countries. *Progress in Physical Geography*, **11**(2), 246–59.
Bowonder, B., 1985. Strategies for managing environmental problems in developing countries. *Environmental Professional*, **7**, 108–15.

Boyle, S. and J. Ardill, 1989. *The Greenhouse Effect*. Hodder and Stoughton, London.

Brown, L.R., 1986. *State of the World, 1986: A Worldwatch Institute Report on Progress Toward a Sustainable Society*. W.W.Norton, New York.

Brown, L.R. and P. Shaw, 1982. *Six Steps to a Sustainable Society*. Worldwatch Paper no.48.

Bull, D., 1982. *A Growing Problem: Pesticides and the Third World Poor*. Oxfam, Oxford.

Bunyard, P. and F. Morgan-Grenville, 1987. *The Green Alternative: Guide to Good Living*. Methuen, London.

Button, J., 1989. *How To Be Green*. Friends of the Earth/Century Hutchinson, London.

Carson, S. McB., 1978. *Environmental Education: Principles and Practice*. Edward Arnold, London.

Cottrell, A., 1978. *Environmental Economics*. Resource and Environmental Sciences Series, Edward Arnold, London.

Croxall, H.E. and L.P. Smith, 1984. *The Fight for Food: Factors Limiting Agricultural Production*. George Allen & Unwin, London.

Eckholm, E., 1979. *The Dispossessed of the Earth: Land Reform and Sustainable Development*. Worldwatch Paper no. 30.

Edington, J.M and M.A. Edington, 1977. *Ecology and Environmental Planning*. Chapman & Hall, London.

Elkington, J. and J. Hailes, 1988. *The Green Consumer Guide: From Shampoo to Champagne – High Street Shopping for a Better Environment* Victor Gollancz, London.

Elkington, J., T.Burke and J. Hailes, 1988. *Green Pages:The Business of Saving the World*. Routledge, London.

European Commission, 1987. *The State of the Environment in the European Community, 1986*. Commission of the European Communities, Brussels.

Fang, L., K.W. Hipel and D.M. Kilgour, 1988. The graph model approach to environmental conflict resolution. *Journal of Environmental Management*, **27**, 195–212.

Fernie, J. and A.S.Pitkethly, 1985. *Resources:Environment and Policy*. Harper & Row, London.

Fraser, N.M. and K.W. Hipel, 1988. Using the DecisionMaker computer program for analyzing environmental conflicts. *Journal of Environmental Management,* **27**, 213–28

Goldsmith, E. and N. Hildyard, 1988. *The Earth Report: Monitoring the Battle for Our Environment*. Mitchell Beazley, London.

Gosselink, J.G., E.P. Odum and R.M Pope, 1974. *The Value of a Tidal Marsh*. Center for Wetland Resources, Louisiana State University, Baton Rouge. LSU-SG–74–03.

Gradwohl, J. and R. Greenber, 1988. *Saving The Tropical Forests*. Earthscan, IIED London.

Grainger, A., 1982. *Desertification:How People Make Deserts, How People Can Stop and Why They Don't*. Earthscan, IIED, London.

Haigh, N., 1984. *EEC Environmental Policy and Britain*. Environmental Data Services Ltd, 40 Bowling Green Lane, London EC1R ONE.

Hallsworth, E.G., 1987. *Anatomy, Physiology and Psychology of Erosion*. Wiley, Chichester.

Ham, S.H. and D.R. Sewing, 1988. Barriers to environmental education. *Journal of Environmental Education*, **19**(2), 17–24.

Ham, S.H., M.H.Rellergert-Taylor, and E.F. Krumpe, 1988. Reducing barriers to environmental education. *Journal of Environmental Education*, **19**(2), 25–34.

Harrison, P., 1983. *The Third World Tomorrow*. Penguin, London.

Harrison, P., 1987. *The Greening of Africa: Breaking Through in the Battle for Land and Food*. Paladin, London.

Hughes-Evans, D., 1977. *Environmental Education:Key Issues for the Future*. Pergamon, Oxford.

International Institute for Environment and Development/World Resources Institute, 1987. *World Resources 1987*. Basic Books, New York.

International Institute for Environment and Development/World Resources Institute, 1988. *World Resources 1988–89*. Basic Books, New York.

Khoshoo, T.N., 1984. *Environmental Concerns and Strategies*. Indian Environmental Society, PO Box 7033, New Delhi 110002, India.

Lees, A. and K. McVeigh, 1988. *An Investigation of Pesticide Pollution in Drinking Water in England and Wales*. Friends of the Earth, London.

MacIntrye, A.A., 1987. Why pesticides received extensive use in America: A political economy of agricultural pest management to 1970. *Natural Resources Journal*, **27**(3), 533–78.

Myers, N., 1987. *The Gaia Atlas of Planet Management*. Pan, London and Sydney.

Odum, E.P., 1976. The coming merger of ecology and economics. Paper presented at the Forging the Economic Quality of Life in Georgia seminar. Georgia Center for Continuing Education, Athens, GA. 26 March.

O'Riordan, T., 1976. *Environmentalism*. Pion, London.

Owens, S., 1989. Integrated pollution-control in the United Kingdom:prospects and problems. *Environment and Planning C: Government and Policy*, **7**, 871–91.

Pearce, D., A. Markandya and E.B. Barbier, 1989. *Blueprint for a Green Economy*. Earthscan, IIED, London.

Porritt, J. (ed.) 1987. *Friends of the Earth Handbook*. MacDonald, London.

Porritt, J., 1988. *The Coming of the Greens*. Fonatana/Collins, London.

Robinson, S. (ed.) 1986. *Healthier Profits, Business, Success and the Green Factor*. The Environment Foundation, Ibex House, Minories, London, EC3N 1HJ.

Saetevik, S., 1988. *Environmental Cooperation between the North Sea States*. Belhaven Press, London.

Sandbach, F., 1980. *Environment, Ideology and Policy*. Basil Blackwell, Oxford.

Schwarz W. and D. Schwarz, 1987. *Breaking Through: Theory and Practice of Wholistic Living*. Green Books, Hartland, Bideford, Devon, EX39 6EE, UK.

Seymour, J. and H. Girardet, 1987. *Blueprint for a Green Planet: How You Can Take Practical Action Today to Fight Pollution*. Dorling Kindersley, London.

Singer, A., 1987. *Battle for the Planet*. Pan, London

Stokes, B., 1978. *Local Responses to Global Problems: A Key to Meeting Basic Human Needs*. Worldwatch Paper no.17.

Timberlake, L., 1985. *Africa in Crisis: The Causes, the Cures of Environmental Bankruptcy*. Earthscan, IIED, London.

Trudgill, S.T., 1989. Environment today: Forests for people. *Geography Review*, **2**(3), 29–32.

Wang, M., K.W. Hipel and N.M. Fraser, 1988. Resolving environmental conflicts having misperceptions. *Journal of Environmental Management*, **27**, 163–78.

Index

* Numbers in italic = main items of a group